REFLEXIVE SELF-CONSCIOUSNESS

THE COLLECTED WORKS OF

EUGENE HALLIDAY

Volume Two

REFLEXIVE SELF-CONSCIOUSNESS

Melchisedec Press

Melchisedec Press

5 Taylor Road, Altrincham, Cheshire WA14 4LR
melchisedecpress.net
info@melchisedecpress.net

Fourth edition (revised) published in the UK by Melchisedec Press in 2019

Edited by David Mahlowe (1989) and Hephzibah Yohannan (2019)

The rights of Eugene Halliday to be identified as author of this work have been asserted in accordance with Copyright Designs and Patents Act.

The moral right of the author is asserted.

© Hephzibah Yohannan 2015
Cover illustration by Eugene Halliday
Cover design © Hephzibah Yohannan

All rights reserved.

This book is sold subject to the condition that it shall not, by way of trade or otherwise, be lent, re-sold, hired out or otherwise circulated without the publisher's prior consent in any form of binding or cover other than that in which it is published and without a similar condition including this condition being imposed on the subsequent purchaser. Nor shall any part of this publication be reproduced, stored in a retrieval system or transmitted in any form or by any means without the prior permission in writing of the publisher. Permission can be obtained through Melchisedec Press

ISBN 978-1-872240-01-5 (1989 hardback)
ISBN 978-1-872240-39-8 (2019 paperback)
ISBN 978-1-872240-40-4 (2019 ebook)

The Melchisedec Press was founded by David Mahlowe
to publish the works of Eugene Halliday

Printed and bound by Ingram Spark
Set in Baskerville

Dedication

Dedicated to the memory of David Mahlowe
with grateful thanks for his loving and unstinting labour
in the furtherance of the work of Eugene Halliday

REFLEXIVE SELF-CONSCIOUSNESS

Contents

Editors' Notes	ii
Illustration by Eugene Halliday	v
Author's Prologue	1
Reflexive Self-Consciousness	8
About Eugene Halliday	49
Acknowledgements	51
Further Reading	52
Books by and about Eugene Halliday	63
Listen to Eugene Halliday's Lectures	66
Further Information	66
Index	67

Editors' Notes

David Mahlowe 1989

This short work is the highly compacted seed-kernel of Eugene Halliday's teaching. It informs all his writings, and the psycho-therapeutic techniques which he developed, and through which he helped so many towards reflexive self-consciousness.

He believed that as the human mind grows in experience, it becomes more self-stimulating and less dependent on outside sources for its evolution. Ultimately, it is capable of generating from within a microcosmos which is in direct correspondence with the macrocosmic intelligence. This constitutes the state of reflexive self-consciousness, the highest level of individual development.

Hephzibah Yohannan 2019

Eugene Halliday wrote this book, the second of his published works, in the 1950s. It was first published by the International Hermeneutic Society (IHS), and again with the same text by the Institute for the Study of Hierological Values (Ishval) a decade or so later. David Mahlowe, Halliday's Literary Executor, founded The Melchisedec Press to publish Halliday's work. He edited and published this work in hardback, in 1989.

This new edition gives the text of Mahlowe's 1989 edition together with the restoration of missing passages from the original IHS edition. Occasionally a paragraph, sentence or part-sentence found in the original edition was omitted from the 1989 edition, or a different word was used. It is not known whether these variations were chosen by the author or by the editor, or whether they may have been simple omissions or variations due to retyping. In certain instances an editorial choice has had to be made between slightly different words, or variations in punctuation, occurring in the two versions; this in no way affects the meaning of the text. The most notable of these is in the fourth sentence of paragraph 30 (page 7): the word 'concepts' in the 1989 edition may have been a transcription error, as the word 'percepts' in the IHS edition makes more sense in the context of the paragraph; the word 'percepts' has therefore been chosen for this edition.

Words emphasised in bold in the original softcover edition were rendered in italic in the 1989 hardback edition; here they have been rendered in bold. Some italicizations were added by David Mahlowe in the 1989 edition for clarity and emphasis, and have been rendered in bold here, for consistency; for example in paragraphs 241–246 (pages 45–46). In this edition italic has been used for non-English words such as Latin or Greek.

Single quotation marks have been chosen for this edition rather than double, for consistency of style across the new series of books published by Melchisedec Press since 2015.

Page numbers in centred square brackets within the text indicate the page numbers of the hardback edition, e.g. [page 1]. They are placed as close as possible to the end of each page, without breaking paragraphs (for ease of reading). This has been done so that a forthcoming Index to Halliday's Collected Works may be used with this new edition; and so that students discussing or citing the work may be able to reference the pages of the hardback. Each paragraph has been given a number in square brackets, to further facilitate the referencing process.

Reflexive Self-Consciousness
by
Eugene Halliday

Author's Prologue

[1] Before entering into the discussion of our subject we will quickly examine a few terms relating to consciousness. There are several words often used more or less indiscriminately to express what we mean when we say we know anything; and as knowing is known only to a knower, **words relating to knowing are not definable ultimately other than by appeal to the knowingness in a knower.**

[2] We may say we know a thing, we are aware of it, we are conscious of it, we feel it, we sense it, etc..

[3] Awareness, consciousness, feeling, sensation; all these words refer to that whereby we know what we know. It is significant and important that we cannot indicate what we mean by one of these words without appealing to that in us which corresponds with their significance, that is, to that in us which **knows** that it knows. From this fact may be shown the ultimate infiniteness of sentience.

[4] All these words refer to that in and by which we know. If we persist in asking what we mean by this we can reply only, 'We **know** what we mean. Consciousness is its own evidence. Self-evidence is the means whereby sentience knows itself'.

[page i]

[5] Because it is not proved by other than itself to itself, we say that consciousness of consciousness is immediate. 'Immediate' means 'not mediated', not using anything other than itself to know itself.

[6] Nothing proves consciousness or sentience to exist other than itself. But the existence of objects in consciousness is proved only by consciousness. Without consciousness or sentience, even if objects existed, there would be no actual proof of their existence.

[7] Although the words 'consciousness', 'awareness', etc., all refer to that in and by which we know things, we may distinguish some difference in their usage.

[8] The word expressing what is most basic in the knowing process is 'sense', a word derived from the Latin *sentire*, **'to feel'**.

[9] We know what we mean when we say we feel. Feeling is basic in the sense that of ways of knowing it is general rather than special, universal rather than particular, undefined rather than defined. A feeling is less clearly outlined than an idea, although a feeling of pain may be sharply localised. We may say that feeling is our state when we know the field of our experience: feeling is field-awareness. To feel is to know a field-state.

[10] A field in electronic theory is defined as a zone of influence of a force. Psychologically, we may say, a field is a zone of feeling, or a place in which we feel some process, or sense something, without defining precisely what form it has. In principle a field is ultimately infinite. The field of sentience is limitless.

[page ii]

[11] The Latin-derived word we may use for feeling is 'sentience'. It has a less particularised use than 'consciousness', and therefore may be used to express that faculty in us whereby we know by feeling. By 'sentience' we shall mean that which knows by feeling without sharply defined formal content, but which is the ground of the possibility of formally defined consciousness.

[12] The word 'consciousness' has a more specific significance. It is from the same root as 'science'. The 'sci' in the word is seen in the Latin *scindere*, **'to split, to separate'**. Consciousness knows things as separate from each other. Consciousness defines analytically what sentience experiences wholly and non-analytically. (One of the most efficient ways of developing consciousness is by verbalisation, for words help towards analysis of the content of consciousness.)

[13] The word 'awareness' is derived from the Old English *waer*, **'cautious'**. It is cognate with the Latin *vereri*, **'to observe anxiously'**. To be wary is to be on guard in feeling, to be watchful.

[14] Rather amusingly, the other word 'ware', meaning **goods or merchandise**, is connected with the Old Norse *vara*, meaning **'skin or fleece'**. No doubt in former times (!) it was occasionally necessary to beware of the ware-sellers in the market-place in order to avoid being 'fleeced'.

[page iii]

[15] Awareness then, we might say, carries with it a sense of being on guard. Consciousness or sentience qualified by caution.

[16] All these words may be used interchangeably, with occasional preference for one or the other according to the requirements of the context. All refer to that in and by which we know what we know and **that we know**.

[17] The objects in the field of sentience are limited or finite. The field itself is not. Every thing, every definable idea, every temporary feeling-state or emotion, may be considered as a finite datum within a sentient field, itself infinite.

[18] The field must be said to be infinite, because every limited object in it may be represented by a circle, and every circle, no matter how large, may have another larger circle drawn round it, and so on to infinity. The environment of a thing is always larger than a thing, and is in principle ultimately infinite.

[19] The infinite sentient field must be conceived to be the source of all beings, for the fact of being is a fact only to consciousness, and however abstract thought may try to eliminate consciousness from being, it experiences no being other than in and of consciousness.

[page iv]

[20] When we consider the ultimate source of all beings, we are forced to conceive it as such a source which has given rise to beings of our own order, that is, conscious beings.

[21] There is a peculiar fact about sentience, or awareness, or consciousness. If we exclude it from the ultimate source of being, if we do not posit it as a property of that source present from the very beginning of creation or evolution, we cannot find a point later at which we may logically introduce it. Sentience denied at the source of being cannot be later introduced into the stream flowing from it.

[22] Attempts have been made by materialists to exclude consciousness from the source of being, and then to try to explain its presence in ourselves by saying that it has arisen by the aggregation of

non-conscious material particles into complex patterns, like those we know in our nervous system and brain-structures.

[23] Of this we assert, that whilst the complex brain-cell aggregate we possess may be patterned in such a way as to provide our consciousness with a machine complicated enough to serve as a vehicle for the expression of the complex processes of consciousness, if the brain is considered to be merely an aggregate of non-conscious material particles it cannot of itself give rise to consciousness. If each material particle is non-conscious or insentient, then the mere placing together of a large number of such particles, however arranged, cannot give rise to consciousness. If a material particle is a not-knower, then a million million like it cannot add up to a knower. No number of zeros ever adds up to more than zero, no matter how we arrange them.

[page v]

[24] The ultimate source and origin of our being is sentient and conscious. A stream cannot rise higher than its highest point. The consciousness in man cannot rise higher than its own ultimate source, and in the generality has not yet reached so high.

[25] The greatest intellects of the world all bow their heads before the infinite potential of their origin. Only the ignorant lack humility.

[26] To become conscious of our source is to become conscious of the source of all being and all consciousness. It is to become consciousness itself, and reflexively self-consciously so.

[27] To confine our consciousness to the consideration of the finite objects of our five special sense organs is unnecessarily to limit its scope. The sentient field is itself infinite. To concentrate consciousness fully upon a particular object within that field is to deprive oneself of the knowledge of what lies beyond that particular.

[28] To rescue oneself from the self-imposed ignorance of the particularising consciousness, one has only to remove the stress placed by consciousness upon the particular, and replace it in its source.

[page vi]

[29] The particularising tendency of the lower mind is a product of the over-specialising activity of the five special sense organs, an over-activity initially imposed on them by the external stimulus situation. This is presented in the Eden myth by the Serpent which acted on the woman Eve (the feeling and the substance side of man), and so drew into the external world his sense-organs, capturing his mind in materiality.

[30] It does not need a great deal of thought to see that full concentration on a given finite thing deprives us of data beyond it. The mind which merely sees separate particular things, and not their world context, is a mind deprived of universal concepts which could confer order upon his sense data. All contents of consciousness are functions of power. To confine oneself to particular sense percepts is to deprive oneself of the energy contained in concepts of universal validity.

[31] The particularising man, tied to separate, serially-experienced finites, functions at a low level of consciousness. He is tied to the data provided by his five special sense organs. He reacts to stimuli like an animal rather than a rational being. Free-will is to him a term with no other significance than stimulus-reaction, or taxism-response.

[32] The generalising man has begun to free himself from particularised reactions. He has begun to see the Law which governs the world.

[page vii]

[33] The universal thinker carries the work further. His intellect has lifted him to the level where universally true concepts confer upon him power to order the particular and the general.

[34] The absolute man is the man who sees beyond the universe as a formed thing, into the laws of motion which bring it into being. He recognises the relation between these laws and the laws of his own consciousness. He sees all things as produced by motion, and motion as produced by the Absolute, and the Absolute as infinite, eternal, sentient power. And he knows his own consciousness as that Absolute Sentient Power operating through the vehicle of his body. He knows what is meant when it is said, the Universal works through the

particular, the Absolute through the relative. He centres himself in the Absolute even as he operates through the relative.

[35] He does not conceive himself as separate from the Absolute. He says, 'I and my Father are one'.

[36] The absolute man, the man of the Absolute, is the reflexively self-conscious man who has turned his consciousness away from the particulars of the world, in order to become one with the principle of their being. For him, freed from the fixated identification with a particular finite body, there is no 'outside'. All beings are **within** his consciousness. In leaving all things to return to his true self he has discovered all things with himself in the Absolute from which he derived. In losing his life he has found it.

[page viii]

[37] The particularising man is the prodigal son who drove forth from his father's house, and has not yet reached the point of realising that he is eating husks with the swine.

[38] The man who begins to generalise is the prodigal son at the point of his first stirrings of awareness that he has sinned.

[39] The universal thinker is the prodigal son who recognises once more that he stands in his father's house.

[40] The absolute man is the prodigal son sitting with his Father rejoicing in their re-union.

[41] The reflexively self-conscious man knows these things, and more. He knows that reflexive self-consciousness is the beginning and the end of the journey into time and particularity. He knows it is the beginning because the Absolute has always from eternity reflexed upon itself in its own non-difference. He knows it is the end because, after having lost it and entered into the time process, man is driven by the Absolute to regain it. The Alpha and Omega, the beginning and the end, are the same.

[42] In between the beginning and the end stretches the time process, the realm of Saturn-Chronos. Within this process, in this realm, fallen man who has not yet returned must receive the education which

will bring him, the man who in leaving his source left himself, back to himself again in the supreme all-power-conferring act of reflexive self-consciousness and self-realisation.

[page ix]

[43] Once returned, man with his catalytic creative-consciousness, will gaze forth upon those of his brothers who have not yet returned, and by the power of his sentience and reflexive self-consciousness will be able to create in them the awareness of their position, which will place them at the point at which he once stood, the point of decision to return.

[44] In what follows, the words 'consciousness', 'awareness' and 'sentience' will be used more or less interchangeably, although their different significances may conveniently be borne in mind wherever a context justifies it.

E.H.

[page x]

Reflexive Self-Consciousness

[45] The opening of the twentieth century forced into man's consciousness a serious problem. It is the problem of the attainment of adequate powers of reaction and stimulus-assimilation in an increasingly complex life situation, with a continuously accelerating development pace which threatens man's very existence.

[46] Reflexive self-consciousness, which for convenience we abbreviate to 'resec', is a state of transcendent self-awareness which confers upon the beings who attain it certain powers of adequate response and capacities of stimulus assimilation. These powers man must either attain, or perish from the earth as unfit for the next necessary step in the evolution of consciousness.

[47] First we must state the basic rule for the attainment of resec. It is: **THE OBSERVER IS NOT THE OBSERVED.** What does this mean? Shakespeare says, 'The eye sees not itself but by reflection'. When we go to a mirror and look into it to see ourself, we see not ourself but a reflection of our face. A simple fact, yet of tremendous significance.

[48] The eye, of course, does not see of itself. Behind the eye is the ocular brain centre and the observing self. Consciousness of an object arises only if these three are brought into relation and directed to an object.

[page 1]

[49] We can see another's eyes. It is possible that a man might have his nose removed and by violent squinting see his own eyes. But through each eye would be seen not itself but the other eye. The eye which sees does not directly see itself.

[50] Let us apply this physical fact to the problem of the Observer and the Observed.

[51] If we look inside ourself in an attempt to see what we mean by the self, we discover, if we pursue our attempt to the end, that the self is not see-able in any objective sense. The Self is consciousness

itself, awareness, sentience. It is that in which objects may appear, but it is not itself an object.

[52] Consciousness is not an object, not a formed thing; it is that in which objects, things, forms and ideas appear. What follows from this is so deeply significant, so tremendously important for the attainment of freedom, that we must spare a little time to make clear its more important implications.

[53] Somehow consciousness **is**, yet is not so in any objective sense. We know this to be so because we are immediately aware of our consciousness as soon as we turn to it. We say **immediately** aware because our awareness of our awareness is not mediated by anything other than itself.

[page 2]

[54] When we are aware of some **object** through one of our senses, our awareness is mediated through the sense organ. When we are aware of our **awareness**, this awareness is not mediated, and we therefore say it is immediate.

[55] Whenever we use a sense organ to become aware of an object, the sense organ in some degree conditions what we know. When we are aware of our awareness, our awareness is immediate and therefore unconditioned.

[56] To be unconditioned is to be free. Awareness of awareness is therefore free. Consciousness of consciousness is consciousness conscious of itself. This is the key to resec and free self-determination.

[57] Although we say that the Observer is not the Observed, we do not posit thereby a dualism of two different substances, for the Observed is merely a motion-pattern in and of the Observer. The ultimate substance is sentient power. Its motions generated by its power constitute the objective content of its sentience, which brings us to our second important rule for the gaining of resec.

[58] Our second important rule is this: **An Observer knows only the modifications of the Observer**. Let us examine this.

[59] When we are deprived of stimuli, whether external or internal to our organism, the content of our consciousness is reduced. We can see that if we were totally deprived of all objective stimuli, consciousness would have no **objective** content whatever. Such a state of consciousness deprived of all objective content, we call unconsciousness. Unconsciousness is not what people ordinarily suppose it to be. It is simply consciousness with no objective content; that is, objectless sentience.

[page 3]

[60] The Observer is consciousness serving some object. But the object served is simply a form of motion within consciousness. There are no objects of consciousness other than within consciousness as modifications of it. Without modifications in consciousness there are no objects within it, and there is no objective consciousness.

[61] All objects of consciousness, all the things of the world, all ideas and mental states, are simply forms of motion in consciousness.

[62] It is quite futile for a conscious being to posit an existence beyond consciousness. The 'existence beyond consciousness' is merely a concept **in** consciousness. Dr. Johnson's kicking a brick to refute Berkeley is just another evidence of Johnson's obtuseness, and unfitness to deal with the problem.

[63] The Greek philosopher Anaximander saw the source of the world in the everlasting motion (*aidos kinesis*) of that which is limitless or boundless (*apeiron*). This idea is a true one. Each great philosopher has been a doorway for a part of Truth.

[page 4]

[64] When we examine Anaximander's *apeiron*, the boundless source of the world, we see from his choice of name for it that he correctly conceived its motion to be a motion of pure translation, that is a non-circumscribed motion, a motion which did not close itself upon itself. A motion which closes upon itself must, of course, be bounded or finite.

[65] When we consider possible kinds of motions we see at once that we may consider them basically as of two kinds, motions

which close upon themselves, and motions which do not close upon themselves.

[66] Motions which close upon themselves we may call cyclic, circumscribing or rotatory motions. Such motions are symbolised by the serpent with its tail in its mouth.

[67] Motions which do not close upon themselves we may call translating motions. Translation means 'moving from one place to another'. A translating motion is one which moves through space from place to place, without closing itself. It is symbolised by a serpent running freely in wave form.

[68] There is a certain relation between motions of rotation and motions of translation. Both are motions, and motion is a concept we have built from our experience of the change of place of sense objects. We shall deal with this elsewhere.

[69] We know today that material bodies are simply modes of motion. We know that whatever finitely exists must be composed of the motion form we call rotation; for unless the motion is of the type of rotation it cannot circumscribe a boundary in space and thus mark out that space as the place of its being. A non-rotating motion does not locate itself in space and thus cannot bring into being anything characterised by a boundary or formal limit; that is, it cannot bring into being any finite object whatever.

[70] If we think very carefully about what it means to exist, what it means to be a being, we will discover that the idea of being is the idea of a circumscribed zone of action.

[page 5]

[71] What is not circumscribed is not a being properly so-called. Thus the infinite power source of all being is not properly called a being, though all beings subsist in and of it as motion-modalities of it.

[72] Every **actual** being, every being **actually**, is a being constituted by a **form of action** circumscribing and confining itself in a certain place. When action or motion is confined to a definite place it must be considered to be circumscribed. A circumscribing act is a rotating motion.

[73] Without rotation of motion, without a motion circumscribing itself, there would be no being, no existence, no world of stars, suns, planets, plants, animals and men; no thing whatever. Motion of rotation circumscribes, creates and keeps in being all things that exist.

[page 6]

[74] What can we say about non-rotating motion, motion of translation? First we must say that it does not as such bring into being any finite thing or object whatever. Finite beings are constituted, consist of, motions of rotation. A motion of pure translation brings no finite whatever into existence. It is an infinite motion, like the everlasting motion of Anaximander's *apeiron.*

[75] If we conceive the motion of pure translation we do not conceive a finite, we conceive an infinite motion. This infinite motion is like the theologian's concept of the eternal motion of God's will, or the absolute motion of certain of the philosophers.

[76] If we consider a being constituted only of rotating motion with no translation whatever, we are really conceiving a being which can only be an intellectual abstraction, for certain reasons we shall see later. But if such a being could exist, constituted only of the motion of rotation with no translation whatever, such a being would be static and of itself incapable of relation with other beings.

[77] We must here break the inertia of ordinary thought and say that 'static' means merely standing in one place, but that what is 'standing' is simply a system of rotating motion. All standing or static beings are kept in being by motion of rotation, or recurrent cyclic impulses.

[page 7]

[78] If we were to conceive all beings to be static in this way we see that each being would be isolated from the rest. No special grouping together would occur, and thus no complex beings would arise. Thus nothing of the process we call involution or evolution would occur. The dynamic world of complex beings and relations we know would not exist.

[79] But if we conceive motions of translation to be added to those of rotation we see that such motions would confer on beings the possibility of dynamic relations, coming together and separating, integrating and disintegrating, which as beings constituted by mere rotation they could not have.

[80] Motions of pure translational type do not as such bring to be any existential beings whatever. They simply pass through space, leaving no trace or evidence of their passing.

[81] Motions of pure translation are like those attributed to the Absolute, the Infinite Motion presupposed by the existence of the finite things of the world around us.

[82] Why does a finite being imply infinite motion? Because a finite being is a motion of rotation circumscribing itself in space, and beyond every circumscribed zone there is always an infinity of space in which further motions occur.

[page 8]

[83] To illustrate this we draw a circle to represent a zone of rotating motion. No matter how big we make this circle we can always conceive that we might have made it larger. There is always infinite space for us to move in beyond our circle. The larger we make our circle the more its curvature approaches the straight line. The straight line, like the free running serpent, is a symbol of translating motion. It is a line of infinite curvature, that is, a line of no finite curvature.

[84] When we draw a circle, we observe that its line rotates and circumscribes a zone in space. We say that it simultaneously includes and excludes. It includes, or closes in, a finite zone called a place. It excludes, or closes out, an infinity of space beyond. A fact we shall find most important when we come to consider the problem of identification.

[85] The closed-in zone is a place of finite actuality, or an actual being, an existential entity, a reference centre for consciousness, an object on which the will may act.

[86] The excluded infinite is the space of the translating motion. Pure translating motion travels infinitely, that is, to no finite end or limit.

Travelling to no finite limit, not returning upon itself, pure translating motion does not constitute or bring into existence any finite beings; yet all finite or rotating circumscribing motions, which constitute the world of things, exist within and in virtue of the infinite motion of the Absolute, which constitutes the infinite field determining the relational possibilities of things.

[page 9]

[87] The Absolute is an infinite sentient power, an eternal continuum of motion. Because it is sentient it feels its own motion. Its motion is the content of its sentiency. It is from this fact that is derived the principle which says that a being knows only the modifications of its own substance, or consciousness is aware only of its own modalities.

[88] The sentience and motion of the Absolute are not factually separable from each other. It is merely a process of abstractionist thought to consider them so. Sentience and motion are both properties of the Absolute and must be held together in thought with the Absolute. If we conceptually remove either one of them, the universe we know must also be removed. If motion is removed there is no action, no bringing to be of actual things. If sentience is removed there is nothing to know the world. Power is the name given to motion as cause, or to motion as imparting itself to other motion. The word 'cause' is from a Latin word meaning **'to strike'**.

[89] What do we mean by motion imparting itself to motion? The Absolute is infinite sentient motion itself. Absolutely there is nothing other than this infinite absolute motion. What then do we mean when we talk of motion imparting itself to motion?

[90] This is the same question as, What is the relation between the circumscribing motions of rotation-complexes and between these and the motion of translation?

[page 10]

[91] To avoid falling into dualism, which would posit two ultimately different kinds of motion, one of rotation and one of translation, we may draw an image from the behaviour of water.

[92] If we watch any large body of water, say the sea, we observe that the motions which traverse it have a certain character we call undulatory or wave-form.

[93] The peculiar thing about the wave-form motion of the sea is that we know as a physical fact that it is really an illusion. We know that the apparent travelling of a wave over the surface of the sea is really the product of a cyclic motion of the water molecules. Each molecule of water rises and falls about a centre, but is confined in its motions within a very small zone of action. Each molecule's motion up and down, and its slight lateral displacements, are so related to the motions of adjacent molecules that the resultant effect of their motions on an observer is the creation of an apparent wave form travelling across the sea's surface. If we watch a piece of floating wood we see that the motion of the water in that place is more or less a rise and fall without much lateral shift.

[94] We see here that the physically factual motion of the molecules of sea water is cyclic or rotatory, and that such cyclic motions, timed in a certain way, give rise to the appearance of a motion of translation.

[page 11]

[95] We must be on guard at this point not to jump to the conclusion that the physically factual rotatory molecular motion of the water is 'real', and the appearance of the translating wave-form is 'unreal'. For although the translating wave-form motion of the sea may be considered as a mere appearance arising from the rotatory motion of the water molecules, yet rotation itself may be viewed as a special kind of motion of translation, that is, translation about a point. Actually, all motions pre-suppose translation.

[96] Let us examine the concept of motion. The concept arises from the observed change of position of bodies in space. In one moment we observe a body against a certain background. In the next moment we see it again against another background. We explain this phenomenon by saying that either the thing or the background or ourselves as observers have moved.

[97] Our idea of motion arises from the observed change in the relations between a thing, a background, and an observation point; or

between bodies in space; or between contents of consciousness. If we abandon the use of particular observation points or finite bodies, no finite motions are observed as such, and another order of experience of motion arises. What this is, is experienced in the resec state.

[page 12]

[98] In order to measure a motion, we must have certain finite reference points. Such points existentially are what we call bodies. A body is simply a finite zone or place in which certain characteristic motion functions tend to give rise in consciousness to a relatively stable reference point.

[99] Whether we consider a motion as rotating or translating, if we wish to measure it we must posit some fixed reference points from which to make our measurements. Such reference points must, **at the existential level**, be finite bodies; that is, they must be constituted by circumscribing motions, for an existential body owes its existence to rotatory motion.

[100] The concepts of translating and rotatory motions are both dependent on the observation of changes of relative position of reference points in consciousness, points constituting a background, points considered against a background, and points from which observations are made.

[101] The concept of a motion of translation may now be stated as based upon the change of place of a body without reference to any fixed reference point such that the change of place could be considered as having occurred round that point and having returned to its point of original observation.

[102] The concept of a motion of rotation may be stated to be based upon the change of place of a body with such reference to a fixed point that the change of place may be considered as having occurred round that point and having returned to its place of original observation.

[page 13]

[103] Motions of translation and rotation now differ only according to whether they are considered as relative to some reference

points assumed by an observer, and the motion defined in relation to this point as either cyclic or not.

[104] Cyclic or rotatory circumscribing motions constitute finite things. Non-cyclic motions travel infinitely through space. Both cyclic and non-cyclic motions are functions of the Absolute.

[105] Both cyclic and non-cyclic motions, when measured, are so by reference to some relation between a background, a body the change of place of which is to be determined, and an observer's viewpoint.

[106] We can easily see the meaning of the bodies constituting the background and the body whose change of place is to be measured and the body we intend to use as an observation point. They are all points of reference within the field of consciousness, within sentience, within the observer, the self.

[107] What is the observing self?

[108] An **observing** self is simply consciousness focussed on some reference point, sentience centred on an object. Prior to the act of focussing, sentience must be said to be infinite. Sentience is a property of the Infinite Eternal Absolute.

[page 14]

[109] No philosopher has yet succeeded in defining consciousness or awareness or sentience. Why is this so? Because to define is to indicate limits, and sentience as such has no limits. Sentience is not a finite object. It is that in which finite objects are presented and known.

[110] Let us look at the words 'observer' and 'observed'. An observer is a watcher; the observed is what is watched. In order for an observation to occur there must be a watcher and a watched. The watched, the observed, is a finite thing constituted of rotatory motion. The watcher, the observer, is not a finite thing, though he may use a finite thing to observe or to observe through. The observer is not a thing, but that which watches the thing.

[111] No one has at any time seen **as an object** the consciousness which sees the object. In theological terms we would say 'No man has seen God at any time'. In psychological terms we would say consciousness as such never appears to itself as an **object**. Yet in the resec act consciousness is aware of itself; but not as a finite, not as an object.

[112] The observer is the subject who sees. The observed is the object which is seen. The subject is the awareness, the consciousness, the sentience. The object is a finited zone of formal motion within the subject, which stands as the subject's reference point in an act of cognition.

[113] Sentience as such is infinite, being a property of the Absolute. The apparently limited observer, the consciousness in a living body, identified with that body, is limited only by its own act of identification. Identification for all practical purposes confines consciousness to the zone of identification.

[page 15]

[114] Ordinarily we do not take notice of the identification process which ties our consciousness to our body. We simply **fall** into identification. The process of falling into identification is so subtle, so intimately mixed with desire, that we hardly ever stop to consider the nature of it.

[115] The fulfilment of desire, the experience of pleasure, the avoidance of pain; these tend to throw a stress on the pleasure-pain aspects of identification and divert us from the consideration of its more mechanical aspects.

[116] The arising of pleasure from the experience of an object tends to lead consciousness to focus on that object. This tendency is so marked in general that it tends to assume almost the force of a law; sufficiently so in fact to have led many philosophers to formulate a hedonistic view of the universe, that is, a view which states life's aim as the pursuit of pleasure and the avoidance of pain.

[117] This tendency of consciousness to focus on an object the presence of which tends to be accompanied by pleasure or pain, is the greatest misleader of the generality of the race of man.

[page 16]

[118] Not that pleasure or pain as such is bad; but the identification of consciousness with the objects it accompanies leads to slavery of consciousness and the reduction of man to a pleasure-pain mechanism. As such a mechanism he is entirely at the mercy of those beings who know the principles governing such mechanisms. Standing as evidence of this is the great interest of business men and their advisers, and political power-pursuers, in motivational research.

[119] There are degrees of pleasure and pain. These depend on the stimulus-assimilation capacity of the observer's body or his reference centre of identification.

[120] Where the observer's body (note, we do not say the observer himself, that is consciousness itself) is presented with a stimulus which it can easily assimilate, a degree of pleasure is experienced by the identified consciousness. Where the stimulus energy comes in too fast or at too great intensity for it to be assimilated, a degree of pain is experienced.

[121] Whether a stimulus causes pleasure or pain to the identified consciousness depends on the body's capacity to assimilate the stimulus. Everything in the experience of pleasure and pain depends upon the identification of consciousness with a body.

[122] Bodies are limited zones of cyclic motion. As limited, circumscribed zones their energy absorption capacity is also limited.

[page 17]

[123] Stimuli entering bodies are constituted of quantities of motion. Motion considered as operating or working within a closed system is called energy. Finite bodies can assimilate only finite amounts of energy presented at a certain rate and intensity, and in a certain pattern.

[124] Bodies are motion systems characterised in specific ways. If stimuli of the right type are presented at the right rate, that is, put in over a certain length of time, a body may assimilate their motion. If the incoming stimulus motion is in any way wrongly presented, either in formal type, rate or intensity, the body may fail to assimilate it. Such failure implies the disturbance of the body's equilibrium or its possible destruction.

[125] At times of the disturbance or destruction of a body, consciousness identified with it suffers as if it were itself disturbed or destroyed.

[126] How are we to escape the disturbing or destructive effects of excessive stimulus motions on bodies? The answer is short: by non-identification.

[127] No matter how badly stimulus motion may affect a body, if consciousness is not identified with it, it is not affected by it. Identification, and nothing else, is the cause of consciousness suffering pleasure or pain. We say 'suffering' because to suffer is to be in passive relation to something, to allow something to act upon us.

[page 18]

[128] What is identification? It is simply **emotional charge** on a consciousness content. If we view a thing with no emotional charge whatever, if we remove from ourselves all feeling-orientation in relation to an object, we are not identified with it.

[129] What happens if we remove the emotional charge on a content of consciousness? The object becomes for us just a shape, a form with no value. Value belongs not to objects themselves, but to the will. Values are will-stresses.

[130] Value is the stress placed by act of will upon an object or consciousness-content. Even the division of values into intrinsic (inherent physical properties) and extrinsic (sentimental) is itself an act of will. A folk song about the Boll Weevil witnesses this, and receives hearty support from the micro-organisms which attack the Firth of Forth bridge.

[131] Because value rests in will, value can be created or destroyed by act of will. To value is to stress by will. To de-value is to remove such stress.

[132] The God Shiva willed to fold up the universe of things into his third eye. The other gods willed otherwise. They created for him to disturb his concentration a beautiful woman named Maya, (which means cosmic illusion, or the affirmation of substantial activity). They succeeded; for the universe manifestly exists and Shiva wanders blindly through the world to the end of its cycle.

[page 19]

[133] Yet Yogis think highly of Shiva, because at least he knew that value rests in the will, and that the being who can centre himself in himself, centre consciousness in consciousness, instead of in its objects, can absorb the whole of creation into his centre, and thus break the dependence of consciousness on its object and regain original freedom.

[134] We are not to be afraid that the non-identified consciousness will have no content. The content of consciousness is a function of the eternal motion of the Absolute, independent of the identification tendencies of particular beings.

[135] The consciousness which is released from identification with particular objects is not deprived of them. When consciousness no longer identifies itself with objects, they still persist as functions of the absolute motion, but they are seen simply as forms within consciousness, having no power to determine the direction in which new stresses may appear. New stresses ordinarily depend on the previous stress-patterns in the objects with which consciousness has identified. At the resec level consciousness is a catalyst able to initiate action without itself being in any way determined by it.

[136] Consciousness is therefore not to be released from identification with objects in order to annihilate all objects and stand in nothingness. That would be to inhibit the power of consciousness to act as a catalytic formative agent or creative intelligence.

[page 20]

[137] Consciousness is to be released from object-identification in order to be able to return to itself. It is to be released from identification with particulars in order to be able to grasp the universal which confers order upon them. Then it is to release itself from identification with the universal in order to return to its own absoluteness, which contains all things in its own pure motion. 'Seek first the kingdom of heaven, and all else will be added unto you.'

[138] Heaven consists in the equilibration of power, the equilibration of all motion. Identification with particular objects destroys this equilibration.

[139] The disequilibrated man cannot act freely; for he is inclined to follow one course rather than another, and this inclination is bondage. To incline is to take the first step to the fall into identification and slavery.

[140] The bound man is a slave to that which binds him. It matters little what binds him if he is bound, whether he is bound by iron chains in a dungeon, or by ambition and the lust for wealth and power in the world, or by what he mis-calls 'love' for a woman in a dream setting, or by concepts of service to impossible nationalist or political causes. Bondage is bondage, whatsoever form it takes.

[page 21]

[141] Inclination is a tendency to fall into action. The cause of inclination is the emotional resultant of experience and the emotional charge on the experience-records in the body. Every experience is recorded by the experiencing organism.

[142] When an experience-record is re-stimulated, it replays not only the form of the original experience, but also (until it is discharged by the release of consciousness from emotional identification with it) the whole emotional content of the experience.

[143] This emotional content is the agent which orientates the individualised or formally-identified consciousness towards or away from the situation correspondent with that in the experience record.

[144] Within an individual organism the orientation of the psyche (or body-identified sentience) affects the distribution of its

constituent motions, which we may consider as a field of forces, in such a way that its resistance pattern to incoming stimuli and to their outgoing results is altered, and thereby its mode of action or behaviour.

[145] For animals with nervous systems this means the alteration of the pattern of synaptic resistances, which determines the inner destination of an afferent nerve impulse, and the outer direction of the efferent nerve impulse, and its consequent behaviour resultant in the body.

[page 22]

[146] The inclination-determined actions of the body must be considered for all practical purposes as mechanical. The man who acts only from inclination must be considered to be unfree.

[147] We often hear a person say, as if it were evidence of his free will, 'I can do what I want'. But the man who does what he **wants** and yet **cannot determine his wants**, must be said to be a slave to want. An act of free will is not an act of want. Want implies deprivation, lack of something. Free will is a pure positive, lacking nothing. Free will is pure creativity and can bring to be the forms it wills to project. Want is determined by experience-records and their emotional content. Free will is determined by nothing other than itself, and can create its own objects. This is the way the Absolute has brought the world into being, not out of want, or lack, but out of the fullness of its own free will.

[148] Unless a man is able to break identification with the emotionally charged experience-records in himself, his actions will be conditioned by those records. Psycho-analytical procedures aimed to uncover such records and remove from them their emotional charges by leading the patient to 'see through' the situations represented in the records.

[149] Unfortunately there is no guarantee that a given psycho-analytical procedure, even if the procedure is a correct one, will be properly applied in a given confrontation of two psyches in the analyst-patient relation.

[page 23]

[150] Further, although psycho-analytical procedures may have helped some patients in some degrees to re-orientate themselves and adjust to ordinary everyday life and its demands, more than such orientation is required for a man to gain the full control of his response tendencies and attain resec.

[151] The gaining by psycho-analysis of some degree of adjustment to socially necessary relational needs does not of itself confer metaphysical insight into the real nature of consciousness and its objects, or spirit and material beings. Only in properly directed conscious processes involving exercise of will and intellect and feeling is the needed metaphysical illumination gained. For this, in most cases, help and indication of the right direction in which effort is to be made is needed.

[152] We say 'in most cases' because it is true that in exceptional cases, from whatever causes, some beings are able to carry themselves towards resec.

[153] Such, of course, are geniuses; but, if we were to uncover the roots of genius in the long continuous line of protoplasmic evolution, we would find operating even there what the theologian would correctly call 'grace', that is, a capacity in an individual which that individual, considered as a finite being, has not itself created. We here say with the rabbis, 'The fruits such men eat are plucked from trees planted by men they never knew'.

[page 24]

[154] Inclination-determined actions are actions determined by emotionally-charged experience records. Such actions must be considered to be in principle not superior to the conditioned-reflex behaviour of Pavlov's dogs. If actions of this order were the only kind possible for man, we would have to abandon as meaningless the use of all terms referring to the concept of free will. Man would be merely a machine and the evolution of consciousness an illusion. Fortunately this is not so.

[155] It is true that the object-identified man acts as if he were a machine. It is not true that this mode of action is the only one possible for him.

[156] How are we to escape from the determination of inclination and thus rescue ourselves from the mechanical response level of action? How are we to extricate ourselves from the machine?

[157] Shortly, we may say that each one of us must become a deus ex machina, a god outside the machine of the body.

[158] To become a god, if we understand the concept correctly, is not impossible. 'Is it not written', says Jesus, 'Ye are gods?' And, 'Be ye perfect, as your Father in heaven is perfect.' A god is simply a being able from within itself, from its own free will, to determine its own actions towards its good. How are we to become such? The God of gods is the Absolute Infinite Sentient Power which determines its own action towards its own good absolutely.

[page 25]

[159] First we must accept that a being able freely to determine its actions from within itself, is a being not determined by inclinations arising from emotionally-charged experience-records within itself.

[160] A free act, an act of free will, is an act not determined or conditioned by any emotionally-charged experience-records whatever. A free act is an act springing immediately from consciousness not object-identified.

[161] This kind of act is extremely difficult for the object-identified person to conceive. Such a person will say, 'How is it possible to act without being determined by some object? How can I act without regard to the benefit to be derived from my action? And if I move with regard to such benefit, am I not moving by inclination?'

[162] Such a person has not yet grasped the meaning of freedom, of free will, and of the ultimate mystery of grace. The profoundly significant words 'His worship is perfect freedom' have not yet revealed their secret to him.

[163] A free-willed act is an act absolutely unconditioned. It is an act initiated by pure consciousness itself, by the pure awareness of consciousness of its own inscrutable creativity. All original acts spring from this source.

[page 26]

[164] How are we to reach the level where such an act is possible? By breaking free from factors which condition consciousness, by releasing ourselves from object-identification, by conquering inclination ('blessed is he who overcomes'), by lifting consciousness above the level at which conditioned reflexes are brought into existence and operate, or by entering with consciousness into zones of experience-records and discharging their emotional content.

[165] 'Great is he who conquers a city. Greater still is he who conquers himself.'

[166] Identification arises from emotionally-charged experience. Whenever the experience of an object (or situation or event) gives rise to emotion, whether pleasure or pain, and the observer allows himself to focus on this emotion, a tendency arises to react to the object by moving towards or away from it, and to record it as a reference for future orientation.

[167] If, therefore, we do not break object-identification, (and by object-identification in its widest sense we mean identification with any finite content of consciousness whatever) we tend to respond mechanically to situations in a manner determined by the emotionally charged records of our previous experiences, even when they have perhaps merely one element in common with the present extant situation.

[page 27]

[168] To break object-identification we must do four things. First we must see that the object-identified state is a false one, a state which falsely represents consciousness, the subject, as identical with its content, the object. Next we must make clear to ourselves that by allowing ourselves to act by inclination, we reduce our action level to that of Pavlov's dogs, the mechanical reflex level. Thirdly we must see that such mechanically determined responses are incompatible with freedom and human dignity. Finally we must withdraw our will from the experience records and from the pleasure-pain aspects of the content of consciousness, and turn it back upon itself.

[169] This withdrawal of the will from the objects of consciousness and centring of consciousness in itself, the turning back to itself, from the object, of consciousness and will, is the act of resec. So important is this for human evolution and the attainment of freedom and the power to produce an adequate response in every conceivable situation, that if its full import were grasped, the whole effort of humanity would be directed towards its attainment.

[170] Let us look more closely at the idea of consciousness turning back on itself. The Greeks, of course, had a word for it—the word epistrophe, a word surviving as a term in rhetoric for the repetition of the same word at the end of several sentences; as if we were to repeat the word 'consciousness' at the end of every act of perception in order to return consciousness from the object to itself.

[page 28]

[171] In the act of reflexive self-consciousness there is a re-statement of the fact that consciousness is consciousness, not only at the end of an act, but in each moment of consciousness. There is a continuous return or reflexive movement, a bending or turning back upon itself of consciousness during action, such that at no moment does consciousness fall into identification with its objects to the point of losing awareness of its own free essence. Not losing its self-awareness in object-identification, consciousness remains self-immersed in its own free essence.

[172] Let us examine the nature of the self.

[173] Ordinarily when a person says, 'my self', he is not at all clear to what he refers. He tends to think that he means by 'self' a being formed in a certain way, and possessing more or less well-defined and recognisable physical and mental characteristics and behaviour patterns.

[174] But these characteristics and behaviour patterns are not consciousness, not sentience. They are some of the **contents** of consciousness, some of its objects.

[175] The sense of individual separate self-existence, and the ego-sense, arise by identification with form. Body, which stands as the

centre of such identification, is known by its form and mass inertic resistance, a form of motion.

[page 29]

[176] For such identification originally to occur the form must, in being experienced, have been accompanied by some emotional charge. This emotional content of the experience leads consciousness, prior to its gaining the resec state, into identification with it in the attempt to re-experience it if pleasurable, or to note it for future avoidance, if painful. Once identification of consciousness with a given body or motion complex as centre of emotional charge has occurred, identification tends by inertia to continue and maintain itself.

[177] Let us look at the behaviour of consciousness in the case of a man experiencing a sudden great pain to the point of loss of consciousness. Is the loss a loss of consciousness **of** the body or **to** the body? Mechanistic thinkers might say that loss of consciousness is a loss by the body or brain of its consciousness arising mechanically from over-stimulation of the nervous system or brain.

[178] We say rather, the over-stimulation of the body makes it unprofitable for a pleasure-orientated consciousness to remain in a state of identification with the body. This explanation covers more facts than the mechanistic one, including the behaviour of martyrs at the stake, for although their body is over-stimulated, yet because they are not pleasure-orientated they do not lose consciousness, but continue to praise the principle of free consciousness which they worship as God.

[page 30]

[179] If we think carefully about the nature of the self, we realise that by 'self' we do not necessarily mean a physical or other body. Grenfell of Labrador's story of the man who lost both legs and arms yet could still say he was he, most aptly provides an illustration of the non-identity of the self and the body.

[180] Today, with the surgeon's art so beautifully developed, we are not surprised to hear that a man has had some organ of his body removed and replaced with a plastic one.

[181] We can easily conceive an operation or series of operations in which a man's organs are one by one removed and replaced by artificial ones. At each stage of the operation-series, the patient would express his satisfaction with the change of organ. Finally, like the axe fitted with a new blade and a new handle, nothing would remain of the original body. Yet the same consciousness would still be operative through it. The self of man is not the body of man.

[182] What, then, is the Self? Here we use a capital letter to show that the Self to which we refer is not the object-body self careless thinkers think they refer to when they use the word 'self'. The real Self is not a finite body. It is pure free-will consciousness. The implications of this in every field, physical, psychological and spiritual, are tremendous.

[page 31]

[183] The careful thinker, penetrating into his being to discover to what he refers when he uses the words 'I myself' knows that the Self is a free-will consciousness, the ground and possibility and actuality of all being, yet itself transcendent of being. (The word 'being' may properly be used only of what is circumscribed, and consciousness as such is not circumscribed, and therefore not properly called a being.)

[184] Consciousness and will are not two factually separable entities. They are two aspects or properties of the Absolute. Consciousness is that aspect of the Absolute in which objects appear. Will is that aspect of the Absolute which initiates change within consciousness or its objects.

[185] From modern psychological theories the word 'consciousness' has derived a rather restricted meaning. There it is opposed to sub-consciousness or to un-consciousness. We may remove some of these associations by using a less common word, the word 'sentience'. This word implies feeling sensitivity and sense. It is from the Latin 'sentire', to feel, to know.

[page 32]

[186] We will use the word sentience to signify that kind of awareness to which we do not ordinarily attribute verbal formulations.

Sentience is feeling awareness considered apart from any verbalisation process. We may use the word 'consciousness' when awareness is more closely linked to verbal forms. The more clearly anything is verbally expressed, the more conscious it tends to become. Consciousness analyses and synthesises its content.

[187] What modern psychology tends to say about the subconscious and unconscious we will formulate differently. We will say that subconsciousness and unconsciousness are levels of the Self in which verbalisation is either minimal or non-existent for the individual.

[188] There is no absolutely non-sentient level of being. The Absolute source of all beings, the ultimate reality, is itself eternal and infinite sentient motion. Whatever it produces or creates, it does so within and of itself as its functions. Nothing, therefore, exists but in and of the infinite eternal sentient motion, which considered as cause is called power.

[189] The subconscious and the unconscious are therefore not to be thought of as non-sentient, but only as not closely linked to verbal forms, not levels of analysis and synthesis of the contents of the field of sentience.

[190] Verbalisation of experience helps to sharpen and clarify and organise the content of consciousness.

[page 33]

[191] Prior to adequate verbalisation or logical definition the field of sentient motion must be conceived of as in a state of chaotic flux; yet this flux at its own level, viewed as absolute motion, must contain the forms of the infinite wisdom.

[192] In John's Gospel we read, 'In the beginning was the Word; and the Word was with God, and the Word was God.'

[193] The Greek word here used for 'word' is *Logos*. Logos means not just word, but rational word, the ratio of cosmic order.

[194] The Logos of John's Gospel is the formative rationalising motion of the eternal infinite sentient power of the Absolute.

[195] Creation is formulation. Formulation is clarification. Clarification is illumination. The Logos is 'The Light that lights every man that comes into the world'. Which means that every man's consciousness contains the principle of logic.

[196] Let us return to the idea of epistrophe. It means a turning back, a return to oneself. It implies a departure from oneself to an object, and the return of oneself to oneself. It implies the gaining or re-gaining of a lost knowledge of oneself, the re-gaining of self-determination.

[197] The Self referred to is not a body. It is sentient power itself. The Self in the act of reflexion returns to itself. Consciousness, which is not a body, but a knower of the body returns from the body to itself and thus rescues itself from identification with its objects.

[page 34]

[198] The Fall of Adam, the fall in myths generally, refers to the fall into identification with the object world of finite things under the influence of natural stimuli, symbolised by the serpent, which, significantly, acts first through the female side of man's nature, that is, the feeling and body-identified side.

[199] This fall into identification was the beginning of death, for identification with the finite is the death of one's free will and consciousness by its involvement in the phantasy of separativity, which is disintegration or mortality.

[200] The fall into identification with the object world places man under the law governing that world. Only the resec man can truthfully say with Paul, 'We are of the law but not under the law'. We are of the law insofar as we use finite reference points. We are not under the law insofar as we remain free from identification with such points.

[201] The resec man reverses the Fall. He releases himself from object-identification. He turns back from the object to the real Self. He sloughs from himself the pall which fell on him at the Fall and returns to his naked consciousness, beyond all finiting conditions and body processes.

[page 35]

[202] But when he returns to himself the world and its content still remains. The only change, the most miraculously freeing change, is that he is no longer identified with any particular part of it. He has sought the equilibration of power which is called heaven. He has found it, and with it all things have been added unto him.

[203] The resec man sees the same world he saw before, the same world other men see. But he sees it not in the same way. He knows what Blake meant when he said, 'The fool sees not the same tree the wise man sees'. He sees the myriad-branched tree Yggdrasil, but not as other men see it. For he does not fall into identification with any particular branch of it. He sees this tree in the nervous system of the body he uses as a reference centre, as he sees it in the driving radiating forces of macrocosmos.

[204] The resec man sees the world **wholly** without falling into identification with any particular part of it. He is not identified with it, not inclined towards it, not enslaved by it. He can use it, as the Taoist uses an empty vessel to put things in. He can create within it by the catalytic creativity of his awareness, his sentience, his consciousness.

[205] The identified man, on the other hand, in the act of identification, goes under the law which governs the object with which he identifies.

[page 36]

[206] If consciousness identifies with a material body, it goes under the law governing material bodies. So with whatever else it identifies. If consciousness identifies with serial ideational processes, it goes under the formal and logical laws governing those processes. If consciousness identifies with emotional states, it goes under the law governing emotional states. Whatever finite things or processes it identifies with, consciousness goes under the law governing those finites.

[207] Only consciousness identified with itself, reflexive self-consciousness, is free from the law of mechanical action-reaction processes governing all finites.

[208] The word 'reflexion', meaning a binding back, or return to Self, is used anatomically and physiologically of a nerve impulse in a reflex arc. Psychologically and philosophically it refers to the mental process of returning to oneself in meditation or contemplation.

[209] The word 'flex' from Latin *flexum*, from *flectere* 'to bend', is related to the word *falcem* or *falx*, a 'sickle'. The falcon, so-called from its sickle-shaped beak, was sacred to the resec priest-kings of the ancient world. The falcon, the hawk, the eagle, are symbols of the high-flying consciousness which returns to itself as the falcon flies into the eye of the sun, that 'medicinable eye' which brings order to the planets and establishes a hierarchy of powers on earth.

[210] The act of self-reflexion, the motion of pure sentience turning back on itself, releases consciousness from identification with its objects and finite processes and events, and restores it to its original freedom.

[page 37]

[211] *Epistrephein*, the self-relation of the reflexive self-consciousness, is the form of the highest order of being, and sees beyond being into the free spirit of the Absolute.

[212] The material image of this return was seen by the ancients in the orbits and revolutions of the planets. Reflexive self-consciousness returns to its original as the planets return upon their orbits. This is the ground of the Eternal Recurrence which fascinated Nietzsche as it had spell-bound the imagination of the ancients.

[213] But resec does not return, to use a figure of speech, in the same plane with the planets. Its cycle is at right angles to the material plane. It descends into identification with matter in order to experience the finiting processes of that level, and then returns to itself in pure transcendental sentience, awareness and consciousness.

[214] The motion of the Absolute produces within itself the modulations which its sentience experiences as phenomena. Sentient power creates an objective world within itself. It may identify itself with its objectifying motion-complexes, and thus become inertically carried by the necessary mechanical mode of action of their being. In which

33

case we say it is 'under the law'. Or it can retain its self-awareness whilst it is creating, and thus retain its freedom and creative initiative, in which case we say it is 'of the law, but not under the law'.

[page 38]

[215] This retention of freedom and creative initiative is the mark of the resec man, the man who is able to bend back his consciousness upon itself, release himself from object-identification, and thus retain his freedom, even in the middle of the most intense creative activity.

[216] Nothing truly exists in its fullness which is not turned back upon itself. A material body does not exist unless its constituting forces continually turn back on themselves and thus avoid dissipation in space. Consciousness does not truly exist in its fullness until it turns back upon itself in the reflexive act of self-recognition. The consciousness which identifies with its object and becomes fixated upon it, is as if it did not exist for itself. We see this in its extreme form in certain mental disorders in which the patient is so identified with emotionally charged experience-records that he cannot release himself from the identification, and is therefore determined by his experience-records. Such a person may be held in a fixated state as long as the emotional charge on the records is not removed.

[217] A material body, a finite thing, is constituted of motions of sentient power which, insofar as the body continues to exist, rotate within the zone marked by that body.

[page 39]

[218] Insofar as the motions constituting a body are totally closed in upon themselves, the sentience aspect of those motions is held in a state of identification with that body. This state of the total identification of sentience with a closed system of motions is referred to in various ways. The ancients, who knew the value of resec, called the state of total identification with a closed motion system 'Hell'. The same state is also called 'Death', for in it one is dead to the larger possibilities of sentient power. To be 'dead in one's sins' simply means to be so identified with the object of one's consciousness that one is unaware of the infinity of other possible objects or of the meaning of freedom.

[219] Insofar as the motions constituting a material body cannot break out from themselves, the body cannot leave itself. Not being able to leave itself, it cannot return to itself. Thus a body cannot as such become reflexively self-conscious. Return to self-consciousness is not possible for a body as such. Return to self-consciousness is possible only for a non-body, for consciousness itself, for sentient power. The fact of reflexive self-consciousness proves the non-materiality of the reflexive Self.

[220] Reflexive self-consciousness is the highest possible form of awareness. This we may prove by showing that consciousness of an object, without consciousness of the Self which knows the object, is valueless. There is no value for the self in object-awareness without self-awareness. Object-awareness without self-awareness is identification to the point of loss of self, and is equivalent to **being** the object with which one is identified, a catatonic state of object-fixation which reduces the self functionally to the level of a not-self.

[page 40]

[221] All purely mental disorders arise from identification with particular emotionally-charged contents of consciousness. The full return of consciousness to itself in the act of reflexion is the return of health to that consciousness.

[222] Disintegration can happen only to compounds. It can therefore happen to any motion-complex, to material or physical bodies, to ideas, to body or idea-orientated feelings and emotions.

[223] Disintegration cannot happen to sentience as such, for sentience is not itself a compound. It is a pure continuum, an aspect of the Absolute, the field in which objects are presented.

[224] A pure continuum has no parts and therefore cannot fall apart, cannot disintegrate. The consciousness which identifies with the continuum of sentience thus escapes disintegration and death. Thus the release of consciousness from object-identification and its return to itself, is the rising of consciousness above the level at which death or disintegration operate. This is the gaining of immortality.

[page 41]

[225] Objective existence is the product of the motion of the absolute sentient continuum of power. By its modes of motion the continuum produces the forms of actuality we know as the world. Motions of translation intersect, and at their points of intersection produce rotations which constitute the primary points which aggregate together to produce so-called material bodies.

[226] Although the motion of the continuum is necessarily itself continuous, yet it produces within itself by its own translation rotational motions which give rise to the phenomenal world of apparently separate bodies. Bodies, as motion-complexes of the continuum, cannot actually be separate from each other in any ultimate sense. Every body, as a function of the continuum, is influenced by the motions of the continuum and thus of all other bodies. No bodies are completely isolated or insulated from other bodies. All bodies reciprocally interact within the continuum which is the plastic power substance of their being.

[227] In the infinite continuum of sentient power, the Godhead of the theologians, all beings 'live, move and have their being'. The reality of beings is constituted by the functions of this continuum. To identify with this continuum as pure sentience is to return to the Supreme Self. The return of absolute sentience to itself is the return of God to God. The return of the relative awareness of man to the infinite sentience is the return of man to God.

[page 42]

[228] The consciousness in man is the sentience of the continuum in the zone marked by the constituent motions of man's being. This sentience is 'the light that lights every man that comes into the world', and is man's life force, pure sentient power, consciousness and initiative, God in man, the root of what dignity man may possess, and the guarantee of his ultimate return to the Self of selves.

[229] Resec confers upon man the power to be himself; the power to fulfil the imperative, 'Become what thou art', the power to see Time as a function of Eternity, and to act in Time from the essence and form of Eternity.

[230] How are we to gain and retain reflexive self-consciousness? It can be gained only in an act of will in which the will of the self returns to itself.

[231] Ordinarily when one looks at an external object or at its internal correspondent in the mind, one tends, if there is an emotional charge upon it, to **fall** into identification with it.

[232] To a certain degree, identification with an object must occur if one is to become aware of its special character and significance. The psyche must assume the form of the object in the act of perceiving it. Precisely because of this fact is it necessary to free oneself again from the object in the resec act. For if one does not return from the object to the self one remains locked in the object and falls under the law governing the object.

[page 43]

[233] For illustration of this we may look at a man identified with a given functional concept. A soldier is a man identified with such a concept. This concept includes subsidiary concepts, such as obedience to superiors, freedom from ethical considerations when acting under orders ('Yours not to reason why, Yours but to do and die.'), and so on.

[234] Thus when a man is identified with the soldier concept he goes under the law governing beings identified with that concept. He therefore responds to orders from those conceptualised as his superiors, and performs actions which, as a human being not identified with the soldier concept, he would be ethically unable to do.

[235] So likewise with men identified with concepts in other fields of action, the priest, the king, the politician, the business man, and so on. Some concepts have universal application, some have their function only in special fields of action, national, social, institutional, or individual.

[236] A concept is an idea or general notion arising from a group of percepts possessing some common factor. A percept may be defined as a simple act of perception, the presentation of a stimulus, a single act of a sense organ, its correspondent brain centre, and the

psyche conjoined with it. A concept is a group of perceptual elements held together by some similar form.

[237] Just as a percept may possess an emotional charge which inclines the psyche to conjoin with it or not (for a percept is a definite amount of characterised energy having a degree of assimilability for a given organism), so a concept may possess an emotional charge which similarly tends to orientate the psyche towards or away from it.

[page 44]

[238] Concepts, then, as complex formed energy-packets possessing emotional charges, tend to condition the behaviour of the being identified with them.

[239] It becomes clear that, if we are to retain our freedom, we must gain the power to release ourselves from identification with conceptual forms. This power is that we exercise in the act of reflexive self-consciousness, the return of the Self to the Self.

[240] To gain resec a certain exercise must be practised, in principle continuously, in early practice probably intermittently. The exercise itself is simple. But that is not to say that it is, for man in his usual orientation, easy. The battle to overcome the inertia of man's established direction, his generally ego-centred attitude, will not be easily fought. Nor should it be. The prize is too high to be gained easily.

[241] Here is the exercise:— When one is looking at something, or considering an idea or experience, a feeling or emotion, or performing any action, one must say to oneself, '**It is the Self which is consciousness itself which is looking at this thing (or considering this idea, etc.). This Self I am. I return to the Self.**'

[page 45]

[242] On saying, 'It is the Self which is consciousness itself', one must make oneself aware that the Self is consciousness itself, awareness, sentience.

[243] When saying, 'looking at this thing', one must make oneself aware of a directional flow of attention from the consciousness to the thing.

[244] On saying, 'This Self I am. I return to the Self', one must focus oneself again on the consciousness and again become aware of a directional flow of attention, but now from the thing back to the consciousness-self.

[245] This back-flow of consciousness to the Self is what we mean by reflexive self-consciousness. It is the key to man's freedom.

[246] To practise resec is to change the whole quality of one's perception and conception of the world. It is to rescue oneself from identification with the object-world and thus from slavery to the law governing that world. We cannot get lost in the things and events of the world or in ideas or emotional states if we are resec. And when we are not lost we have found ourselves, and the Self of all selves.

[247] The Self of all selves is the Godhead of the theologians, the light and life of all selves, the Saviour of the world from the world. It is the Parabrahman of the Hindus, the Absolute of the philosophers, the centre of every enlightened being.

[page 46]

[248] Without resec one is identified with the content of consciousness, with the things of the world, with ideas of the mind, with the emotional states of the psyche. One is like a man in a dream swayed and submerged in a sea of emotions and half-formed images of the world of phantasy

[249] When we identify with something, some idea, or some psychic state, our consciousness, which is the individuated expression of the sentient continuum of the Absolute, assumes the form of that thing, or idea, or state. Assuming the form of a thing, the consciousness becomes subject for the period of the assumption to the law governing that thing.

[250] To break free from the law which governs the object, one must break identification of consciousness with the object and return to the Self which sees it.

[251] One may identify with the object, with the subject, or with both simultaneously. When one identifies only with the object one goes

under the law governing the object, one apparently becomes the object, acts and reacts like the object. One is enslaved by the object.

[252] When one identifies with the subject only, the object disappears and only the subject remains. The Self is there with no otherness, sentience is there, yet as if it were only a potential.

[page 47]

[253] When one identifies simultaneously with both subject and object, both the Self and its objects exist. Consciousness and its objects appear then as two poles of the Absolute.

[254] But before one can consciously hold oneself in this polarised state of the Absolute, one must return from the object to oneself, from oneself to the Self.

[255] There is a cyclic process of involution and evolution of sentience. Prior to creation, the Infinite, Eternal, Absolute, Sentient Motion or Power is as if it were a mere potentiality (yet only from the point of view of a finite mind trying to conceive it). For itself it is a pure self-actuating motion, 'without shadow of turning', pure translation of spirit, infinite and eternal.

[256] But this pure motion, Self-aware Absolute Sentient Power, by its own essentiality produces within itself (as the motion of the sea produces waves and the intersections of the waves, vortices) the motion modes which constitute the forms we use as reference points for consciousness and which we call bodies.

[257] Sentience, in the place of any given motion mode, tends to fall into identification with it. This is the process of the involution of consciousness into the world of finite bodies.

[page 48]

[258] A finite body is a motion-complex of the Absolute, sufficiently integrated and compacted to present an appearance to consciousness of contoured substantiality. Actually it is a modality of the infinite motion of the Absolute.

[259] Once consciousness has fallen at any given locus into identification with the motion-complex or body in that locus, it has

fallen under the law governing such a motion-complex. It is now conditioned by the motion characteristic of that complex, and reacts to other motions (which now act as stimuli) in a manner determined by its characteristic form. It can now assimilate other motions only insofar as that motion-complex can do so.

[260] Consciousness is then bound to that motion-complex and is affected as we see it in the things around us. In the mineral world it evidences itself only in offering resistance to imposed forces. In the vegetable world it expresses itself in growth processes. In the animal world it expresses itself in instinct and desire-impelled action. In man it expresses itself in rational thought. In the fully developed human being it expresses itself in resec.

[261] From the moment of its first fall into object-identification, consciousness experiences, because the object is finited or limited, a sense of loss of power. This sense of power-loss is the negative aspect of the awareness of the original level from which consciousness fell, presented together with its actual level. In its positive aspect it is the seed of dissatisfaction, called 'divine' dissatisfaction because it impels beings to strive to transcend their actual finite being-level and return to their own proper level in the Absolute.

[page 49]

[262] This divine dissatisfaction is that which drives us from the lower levels of being, abstracts our consciousness from object identification, conducts the evolutionary process of our consciousness, and leads us to resec, the completion of the involution-evolution cycle of our being.

[263] Consciousness, which is sentient power, of itself free, binds itself in the involutionary process to forms of motion within and of itself. The sense of loss of power, the frustration of will which arises in the finite objectified state, generates in its negative phase depression and melancholy. In its positive phase it generates the urge to escape the limitations of the body with which identification has taken place. This urge to escape expresses itself in the evolutionary process by the acquisition of ever more complex action capacities, by means of which consciousness seeks to control its content.

[264] From the Absolute through the relative back to the Absolute; from the subject through the object back to the subject; from consciousness to its content and back to itself. This is the involutionary-evolutionary cycle of the Self of the Absolute, and of man.

[page 50]

[265] The Supreme Self, the original sentient power of the Absolute, consciousness itself, is freed from its objects in the moment it reflexes on itself. Being free from its object, it is free from the law governing those objects. Being free from the law, all things are possible to it. Here one says, 'I can do all things through Christ,' through the Logos-God who has completed the cycle of involution-evolution, who was crucified in matter by identification, who rose from the dead state of the object-identified, who ascended again in the reflexive act of his own consciousness to his source in the Father of all beings, where he 'sits at the right hand of power'.

[266] When the Self reflects on itself only and identifies with nothing else, it is free from everything but itself. No laws of finite things bind it or constrain it to respond to their being. It is itself only, self-determined, free.

[267] To gain the capacity to reflex on oneself at will is to release oneself from bondage to the laws which govern the things of this world. All real freedom stands in this capacity. Without resec, freedom is an illusion, and action is merely re-action to stimuli from the world of things, the world of partials, the un-whole world of separativity and illusory processes.

[page 51]

[268] Either one is a slave or not. Either one is able to give orders to oneself or not. Not to be able to give orders to oneself and to be able to obey them, is to be at the mercy of others. Happy and fortunate is he, who being unable to give himself orders and to obey them, is given the orders of truth and shown how to obey them by one who is merciful. As was Jesus and Buddha and Mahavira the Jina and Lao Tse and Zarathustra and Socrates, and others who have shown the way back to the origin of all beings.

[269] In his relation with other beings in the time process, either a man will rule himself or be ruled by others. Self-rule or other rule. There is no alternative, no escape in this matter from the necessity of choice.

[270] Is it better to rule oneself, or to be ruled by others? To be ruled by others **may** be good—if those who rule know how to and have the true welfare of the ruled at heart.

[271] Jesus talked of good shepherds and bad shepherds. How many sheep have the discrimination to know which shepherds are keeping sheep for the sake of sheep, which for the sake of their wool and which for the sake of their flesh?

[272] There are shepherds who keep sheep for their wool, and the wool is money to buy more sheep for more wool for more money for more sheep for more wool, to infinity.

[273] Unless we can guarantee the good faith and true intent and capability of the shepherds, we had better learn to shepherd ourselves. Self-government is the only really safe government. And self-government is to be secured only by resec. Resec and resec only can save us from the intents and purposes of other beings.

[page 52]

[274] Every man who in history has been truly called great has had reflexive self-consciousness. Resec alone has conferred or ever will confer true greatness on the great.

[275] The truly great man is he who can break through the walls of mass-inertia which bind the world into ever-identical recurring patterns of action.

[276] The time-play of finite things which binds the identified man and blinds him to the true light of his own ultimate self must be seen for what it is. Then man may break its tyranny and return to his free Self.

[277] Samson, when he saw this truth with the eye of his soul, which the enemy had **not** put out at Gaza, pulled down the temple, the temple which symbolises the time-play which identification had built,

and thus returned at last to himself and to his God, the Self of selves from which he will not again go forth to lose himself and find himself bound at the mill with slaves.

[278] Mythos tells in parables to the heart what Logos presents in logic to the intellect, and the senses give partially and serially to the lower mind.

[279] The resec man sees Mythos, Logos and sense data as the three corners of a triangle having its being in the ultimate reality of the infinite eternal sentient motion of the Absolute. To gain resec is to gain the mastery of this triangle and establish one's being in eternity, from which one will 'go no more out'.

[page 53]

[280] And because Time is only the serial presentation of what is established simultaneously in eternity, the resec man sees the eternal form of temporal events and is thereby enabled to react adequately to whatever presents itself to him.

[281] The object-identified man is subject to the law of serial presentation in the Time-process. His action is re-action to a stimulus; and always he is in danger of reacting inadequately, from lack of sufficient data; or too late, from lack of readiness; or too grossly, from the mass-inertia of the body with which he is identified.

[282] The resec man sees simultaneously the events which the object-identified man sees serially. The resec man stands at the causal level of being. Because he sees wholly and not partially, his response is adequate. Because he sees simultaneously whatever is applicable to a given situation, his response is immediate. Immediate adequate response is in the power of the resec man. Solomon might have said, 'With all your getting, get reflexive self-consciousness'.

[283] The ultimate reality of the Absolute is infinite eternal sentient motion. This motion, although itself pure infinite translation, produces by the mode of its self-relation, the rotatory circumscribing motions which constitute the finite things of the world, the objects of perception, the ideas of the mind, the flux of the emotions.

[page 54]

[284] Because sentience is infinite it is extended throughout all space. Whatever motions occur in space are experienced by sentience as the content of its consciousness. Wherever a given motion-complex of a rotatory nature is sufficiently integrated and intense to serve as a relatively permanent reference point, sentience interprets this motion-complex as a body or substantial being.

[285] Wherever the motion-constituents of a given body are such as to give rise to the experience of some degree of pleasure, there is a tendency for sentience to identify itself with that body and strive to keep it in being.

[286] Wherever the motion-constituents of a given body are such as to give rise to pain or unpleasant emotions, sentience at that point strives to inhibit those motions. But in the place of such inhibited motions fear is experienced lest they should break free from the inhibiting forces imposed upon them. Fear is the trembling arising from the conflict of the inhibiting forces and the inhibited motion-complexes, causing pain and unpleasant emotions. The unpleasantness of this fear leads sentience to try to break identification with the zones in which it is experienced. Such zones are walled in or encapsulated and constitute the content of the so-called subconscious.

[287] The totality of such zones of painful and unpleasant motion-complexes constitutes for the sentience trapped in them, Hell. The totality of the motion-complexes which give rise to the experience of pleasure is interpreted by the sentience identified with it as Heaven.

[page 55]

[288] The Heaven of the Absolute, however, is the equilibration of all the motions of infinity.

[289] The Hermetic doctrine says, 'As above, so below, as within, so without'. With the difference that Infinity has infinite assimilation-capacity and response-ability, and the finite has only finite capacity and ability. Hence the necessity of gaining release from identification with the finite and returning to the Self in the Infinite.

[290] At the level of the sentience in object-identified man the motion-complex serving as his body or centre of reference has certain reaction and assimilation capacities of a finite order.

[291] If the motion-complex constituting his reference centre or body receives stimuli resulting in pleasure, the sentience identified with that motion-complex, and which he refers to as his own consciousness, tends to identify with such pleasure and the stimuli producing it.

[292] If the motion-complex receives stimuli resulting in pain or unpleasant emotion, his consciousness tends to try to reject or inhibit such stimuli and resultants.

[293] Thus the sentience identified with any given motion-complex as a centre of reference, whether in man or in any other being, from the particular to the universal, tends to act in similar ways in similar situations, and thus to involve itself in recurrent behaviour patterns—the 'Law of the persistence of error'.

[page 56]

[294] The body-identified sentience in a man, therefore, as a being of finite reaction and assimilation, tends to try to reject or inhibit stimuli productive of pain or unpleasant emotion, and to identify with and preserve in being those stimuli resulting in pleasure.

[295] A man has, therefore, his individual Hell and Heaven within himself. Hell is constituted by motions of inhibited stimuli and their pain and unpleasant emotion resultants; Heaven by the motions of stimuli and their resultants which are experienced as pleasure.

[296] As long as the 'Hell' motions in a man are inhibited and vibrate within him, he lives with a background of fear that they might break out and invade consciousness. In fear of this possibility he strives to keep his consciousness away from them, and place it in those motion-complexes which give rise to pleasure.

[297] But man as a finite system has only finite energies and capacities. He tends like all finite systems to lose energy to his surroundings. When his energies drop below a certain level he has not sufficient to continue the inhibiting process which has kept his 'Hell' motions in subjection. At such times they tend to break out of bondage

and invade his consciousness. Here is the point of his greatest need for the power to break identification with the content of consciousness. But it is also the time when he is least able to do it.

[page 57]

[298] It is not a good thing to allow oneself to fall into bondage. It is a worse thing if, having fallen into it, no attempt is made in the days of one's strength to get out of it. It is the worst thing if, having fallen into bondage, and having made no attempt in the days of one's strength to get out, one finds oneself grown old and too weak to try. Then one stands in danger of taking one's private Hell with one into the next world.

[299] Reflexive self-consciousness confers freedom from object-identification, both with the pains of private hells, and with the illusory pleasures of temporary heavens.

[300] The real heaven, the heaven of the Absolute and the resec man, consists in the equilibration of all powers and all motions. In this heaven there is no fear that an inhibited hell will break forth again, for all things have been assimilated, and man has returned to the true Self in freedom and power.

[301] To become reflexively self-conscious is to become freed from the tyranny of material reactivity. It is to rise above the level of conditioned reflexes, above the level of emotional blockages in repressed complexes. It is to become liberated from the mechanics of serial ideation processes. It is to become truly oneself and at one in intent and essence with the Self of all selves.

[page 58]

[302] And in becoming oneself, and one in intent and essence with the Self of all selves, one does not pass into a characterless misunderstood Nirvana of non-individuated bliss. One becomes what one eternally **is**, a unique centre in and of the absolute sentient power. In the words of Jesus, 'Every man goes into his own place, and his works follow him'.

[303] His cycle of experience completed, the prodigal son who drove forth from his Father's house has returned, and sits with his Father at the right hand of power.

End

[page 59]

About Eugene Halliday

Eugene Halliday (1911–1987), artist, writer, teacher and psychotherapist, was the founder of two educational charities, the International Hermeneutic Society (IHS) and the Institute for the Study of Hierological Values (Ishval—now known as the Eugene Halliday Association).

Hermeneutics is the art or science of interpretation of texts, for example in the fields of religion, philosophy or psychology. It is the means by which these texts are examined to investigate their meaning. Hierology relates to comparative religion, being the study of sacred writings or scripture, and the principles which underlie them.

Deeply versed in hermeneutics, art, religion, philosophy and science, Halliday recommended the reading of the major scriptures of the world and the works of the great philosophers. He taught that the whole visible universe is but a tiny portion of an infinite continuum of power. All worlds, from the great galaxies to the subatomic particles, are subsidiary worlds, or whirls, or whorls, of that same power. That power is omnipresent, that is, it fills all places; it moves and feels its movements—it is sentient. 'God', he said, is a short name for that which he called 'Absolute Sentient Power', or the 'Infinite Continuum of Sentient Power'. We are its activity, its whorls, its rotations. We are not separate from God.

Halliday had a theatrical background, his parents were music hall artistes. What he learned from them would have aided his ability to understand, relate and interpret the wide range of subjects he chose to study. Originally intending to be a violinist like his father, a childhood illness partially paralysed his left hand leading to a change of direction. He attended the Manchester School of Art from 1928 and in the 1930s-40s worked for Allied Newspapers as an illustrator and journalist. He was a conscientious objector in the Second World War and helped others in their tribunals. His work was shown in the Manchester Academy of Fine Art and other galleries, and he began giving talks on philosophy. Soon he became the catalyst for a community of creative people, including refugees from Nazi Germany. This led to the founding of the IHS (1959) and Ishval (1964).

From the late 1950s Halliday devoted more and more of his time to writing, teaching and therapeutic work. He taught that the highest centre of each of us is unique, and how to centre ourselves inwardly so as not to be swept off balance by the pressures of worldly life. One way of achieving this is through a new awareness of language that asks us to make our vocabulary active rather than passive by clearly defining the terms we use, through the study of etymology. His work was to help us to find ourselves, to become independent beings—including being independent of him. His aim was for all those who could rise to it, to become reflexively self-conscious.

Halliday was kind and compassionate—he was a healer whose psychotherapeutic work enabled the recovery of many troubled minds and souls. Yet he almost never gave advice, but taught people how to advise themselves.

He could be a ruthless taskmaster when he saw his students could be inspired to further development. His teaching was esoteric and profound, but also practical. He taught that our true place is in the eternal world, yet he did not despise the time-process, which he explained was essential for our spiritual development. He was a charismatic teacher who embodied the principles he taught and inspired many to follow in his footsteps.

Halliday's work was founded in Love, which he defined as 'working for the development of the highest potentialities of being'. Love, he wrote, 'is a feeling or activity directed at the development of the highest possible functional relationship between beings, an activity which contains, indissolubly bound together, elements of thought, feeling, and will, so that this activity is conducted with clarity, sensitivity, and power.'

Halliday wore his wisdom lightly and had a profound effect on everyone with whom he came into contact. More than thirty years after his death he is still held in affectionate reverence. None of those who met Eugene Halliday could ever forget him, and those who were taught by him regard him as a great sage, a true, reflexively self-conscious being, and a man of great humour and compassion.

Acknowledgements

Grateful thanks are due to the Reading Group of the Eugene Halliday Association for comparing the texts of the original IHS edition of the book with the edition published by Melchisedec Press in hardback in 1989; and for identifying a number of variations and omissions from the later edition. Many thanks to Sheila and Robert Taylor for re-typing the book, indicating the variations and including the omissions, and for proofreading this new edition. Many thanks to Bob Hardy for the idea of numbering each paragraph in the book; this makes it easier for those discussing the book to find relevant passages.

Further Reading

For those new to the work of Eugene Halliday, the first five chapters of his *Contributions from a Potential Corpse*, Book I, are a good introduction to his work (see below).

For further information on the work of Eugene Halliday, visit Melchisedec Press, including the Links page.

Contributions from a Potential Corpse

(The Collected works of Eugene Halliday, Volume Four, Book One)

by Eugene Halliday

(extract)

In his Editor's Note for this book, which he published in 1990, David Mahlowe wrote:

'The first book of Contributions From a Potential Corpse was written in the late 1950s as the beginning of the author's magnum opus. The opening five chapters are conventional in form, if not in content. Thereafter, the remainder of this Book and all succeeding Books [under this title] become more episodic in form

'Over the years, right up to his death in 1987, Eugene Halliday continued to write "Contrib", as he called it, as time allowed. The result may be called a Day Book of Wisdom. It contains the essence of his teaching, clearly set down and copiously illustrated in a manner fondly familiar to those who worked with him. ...

'The Foreword to the Book is, in fact, part of the MS. It is placed at the beginning as a fitting reminder of the author's purpose .

'Contributions From a Potential Corpse is a manual of self-development for Everyman; and a unique treasury of wisdom.'

Author's Foreword

[1] What drives me incessantly to think, to read, to, write? The will to love. Nietzsche says 'the will to power'. But I say that the will to power is perverted love, and that love wills to love, and that love is work for the development of the functional potentialities of being, infinitely. Not power as such, but functionality is the aim. Power has no significance unless it is expended in function. But function has significance even if power as power is never felt to be present in it.

[2] And all function is interfunction. Petrol in the car interfunctioning with electrical sparks, cylinders, pistons, crankshaft, transmission, road-wheels, roads, journeys; men seeing new sights, hearing new sounds, constructing new patterns of significance.

[3] There is no function that is not interfunction, though isolating fools may believe or hope otherwise.

[4] Involve ever more interfunctions with each other, and so create ever more complex and higher interfunctions. This is love ever-expanding, love with no ceiling to its attainings.

[page iii]

[5] I see that people who believe that function can be function without interfunction are leading very narrow and shallow lives. I am determined to broaden them, and deepen them. How I shall do this is through the word, written and/or spoken. Let the Word of God help me, or help Himself through me. For surely men are an irritant to God as long as they try to function without inter-function.

[6] Is it possible for men to impede God? Yes, but He is not without power of response to their impeding activities. He has His prophets, his messengers and His Son, by the sacrifice of whom He can present men with a stimulus they will find it hard to assimilate without reaction of some kind. God has the whip-handle. Man, each man, is the whip-lash wherewith God can scourge all men, until they of themselves will to co-operate.

Eugene Halliday

[page iv]

Chapter 1

[7] With the possible exception of some few persons mentioned in tradition as having passed from this world without being dead at their time of departure, it appears that most people who have been born have later died, and that on statistical grounds alone it is probable that most people born and now living will also die at some time in the future.

[8] For most practical purposes, then, it is probably not too foolish to accept the Buddha's observation, and to assume that we shall, having been born, at some point of time die. For myself the idea of dying holds no terrors, because in the sense that I use the term, dying is a process that can apply only to compound bodies held together, not of necessity, but of temporal pattern processes which might well have been other than they are.

[9] To die is to disintegrate, to fall apart, to undo a pattern of elements once brought together in time past by forces having their origin in the ultimate field of power which creates, sustains and dissolves all things. That my body, having been assembled from various sources, from food, from radiation and so on, will probably at some time dissemble does not surprise me in the least. Assembling and dissembling processes are both equally understandable.

[page 1]

[10] What is important is not the probability of my death but the contributing by myself of whatever is valuable from my experience during the period of my assembling. If death is highly probable for born beings, it may be asked of what value is the experience of life to anyone? I must answer from my experience of life.

[11] Life, between birth and death, is a process, a series of actualisings of being, experienced by what I shall call sentient power.

[12] By sentience I mean the principle of all consciousness, awareness, knowing-feeling. The Latin word 'Sentire' to know, to feel, the origin of words like 'sense', 'sensitivity', etc., expresses the general idea of the function which exists in us as the ground of all our self-

consciousness and knowledge, whether of thought, feeling, will or action, physical or otherwise.

[13] 'Sentience' is a word used less often than the words consciousness, knowingness or awareness, and therefore will serve to express the general activity which the other words express more precisely.

[14] Consciousness, for instance, has the rather precise meaning of knowing things in a patterned way. It is used of knowing when it is fairly clearly defined; knowing in which sense elements, the data of the five senses, are cut out from their back-ground, held in relatively sharp focus and integrated together to form a significant pattern of forms.

[page 2]

[15] In the life-process, between birth and death, or conception and death if you prefer it, experiences show certain differences. It is these differences which suggest that my contribution to life may not be without value to others.

[16] The differences of experience may be divided into categories. There are differences of physical action, of will, of feeling, of thought and so on. There are differences of pleasure and pain, of hope and fear, love and hate. It is these which induce me to write.

[17] What I have to say about them I shall say as clearly as possible, for clarity is one step towards efficiency (cold word, but not cold meaning when properly understood.)

[18] All the troubles of man's world arise from inefficiency, from failure to respond adequately to the situation in which he finds himself. Failure to understand what makes things work, what motivates life; failure to understand what to do about failure to understand. 'With all your getting, get understanding', says the wise old man, looking back on his ill-informed youth.

[19] The way to understanding is the way to that which stands under all things, the way to the ultimate substance upon which the world of appearances casts its deluding shadows.

[page 3]

[20] To understand is to go below the superficial appearance of things, to go down to their root causes, to see the substantial reality which underlies the play of forms which present themselves to our senses.

[21] But why should we bother to go down to the ultimate root of things? Is it not good enough for us to live and enjoy ourselves without seeking to descend into the causes of life and enjoyment?

[22] Yes, of course, if we can do it. Perhaps there are some who do. Whatever is clearly conceivable in all its parts and functional relations is possible. So there may be somewhere some being or beings actually living and enjoying life. For a time. But if such exist, it is not for them I write, except perhaps to provide them with further amusement.

[23] For those, however, whose living is not all joyful, I present the fruits of my own experiences of the life process, and show how, after many attacks on the dragon which guards the tree of life from the unworthy, it is possible to eat once more the fruit that everyone desires.

[24] It is a peculiar thing, a strange thing, that the greatest and most valuable things are also the simplest. It is also a peculiar and strange thing that these simplest and most valuable things have been known to man from his first appearance on the earth.

[page 4]

[25] The myths and legends and fairy stories of the ancient world contain these simple valuable things expressed in a manner once easily graspable by the mind of man; graspable because his thought proceeded naturally in a mythic way. Long before Aristotelian logic began to cripple man's intuition his thought was illuminated with flashes of insight into the nature of reality.

[26] Modern science, too, has flashes of insight into the nature of the world, or more accurately, certain intelligent men of science do. For science itself is only an abstract idea, except in the minds of the

men who devote themselves to incarnating in themselves its principles and the knowledge derived from their application.

[27] There is something man has known about himself from his beginning which still stands as the basis of anything else he may know or come to know. It is the simple fact that he has a body, a vehicle of experience, an organism through which the world acts upon him, and by which he acts upon the world.

[28] This body, this vehicle of experience, is the material basis of the possibility of all the activities which man has called valuable. From this we may formulate our first law of life.

[29] 'Do not prematurely destroy the vehicle of your experience'.

[page 5]

[30] The Almighty has set His canon against self-slaughter. This great law is to be fulfilled as the pre-condition to the fulfilment of all other laws.

[31] Why do I say 'Do not prematurely destroy the vehicle of your experience'? Because this vehicle is the only one one has with which to develop oneself to the level where personal freedom becomes a significant reality.

[32] Depression and misery are not so rare in the world that we can ignore their ill effects. Suicides are not so uncommon that we can reckon them of no account on the scale of the human race. It is not always those of low intelligence who destroy themselves. Many intelligent persons have been led by depression to destroy their material means of communicating with us. Often if these self-destroyers had waited a while, a new situation would have presented itself, a new idea, a new feeling, a new will would have arisen. The world would have changed and brought with its change a new possibility and hope of new life.

[33] Something must be said of the real purpose of life to help those who have lost its purpose, or those who have never known its purpose.

[34] What is the purpose of life—the true purpose? Goethe has defined the truth as 'that which is fruitful.' Let us reframe our question; What is the most fruitful purpose of life? What is a fruit? It is the end result of a growth process which contains in itself the potentiality of further growth and further fruiting to infinity.

[page 6]

[35] What is life? Life is a function of love, an activity in which the potentialities of being are actualised, sustained, developed and transcended to infinity.

[36] Life involves sentience and power incarnating, self-embodying, self-objectifying. Life implies love, and praise and bodily existence, of whatever substance the body may prove to be. The German words *lieben*, to love, *leben*, to live, *loben*, to praise, and *leib*, body, hint at this more clearly than our own mixed English words.

[37] Life is Love embodied and praising all things worthy of actualisation.

[38] What is love? Love is the working for the development of the potentialities of non-being into being, the actualisation of potentials which would otherwise remain unrealised, the manifestation of orders of being which would otherwise remain wrapped in chaos.

[39] Well, supposing the potentialities were to remain unactualised? Supposing orders of being remained in chaos, what then? Would it be bad? Would it, as our materialistic age says, matter? Let us return to the consideration of the ultimate substance of reality.

[page 7]

[40] The ultimate source of all things is sentient power, an infinite ocean of power which feels itself. This is what Hamlet intuited

when he said, "Aye, there's the rub." For as this ultimate source of things feels itself, and as it is absolutely indestructible, an eternal, infinite self-sentient power, what it does is most important to it. For what it does constitutes for it the content of its own consciousness. If it does well, it feels well; if it does ill, it feels ill. The mode of action of the infinite sentient power source conditions that sentient power, determines its formal experience, its joy and pain, its self-activating and suffering.

[41] To die to the material world is not absolutely to cease to be. Nothing can ever cease to be absolutely. The ultimate reality is eternal indestructible sentient power. This being so, to die is at most but to sleep. "And in that sleep what dreams may come must give us pause."

[42] To die is to disintegrate. Dying is possible only for a pattern of forces which has at some point in time integrated itself. Because it has come into being by integration of forces or motion-patterns, so it is possible for it to cease to be by simply disintegrating again. To the born death is certainly a possibility. But the disintegration of a pattern of forces is not the absolute cessation of those forces beyond the pattern. All forces are motions of the absolute sentient power. This sentient power is a continuum. A continuum is not made of discrete or separate parts which may be severed from each other. A continuum is a seamless indestructible whole, not subject to disintegration. (The seamless garment of Christ symbolises the continuum of the Infinite Sentient Power in eternal motion.)

[page 8]

[43] The eternal, infinite sentient power, source of all beings, cannot itself ever cease to be. 'Whatever truly is can never cease to be', says the Bhagavad Gita, 'whatever is not, can never come to be.'

[44] Because it can never cease to be, the infinite sentient power has a problem, somewhat like that presented to Hamlet. But whereas Hamlet's problem is 'To be or not to be', the problem for the infinite indestructible sentient power is, 'To act or not to act'. What it is, it is. This is unavoidable; but what it shall do or not do constitutes its problem.

[45] In the great religions the infinite eternal sentient power is called 'God'. God is said to be omnipotent, all-powerful. It is said, therefore, that to God's omnipotence all things are possible. But for the all-powerful God there is one impossible. God cannot cease to be Himself. He, the eternal infinite sentient power, indestructible source of all beings, can never cease to be Himself. Thus, as He cannot cease to be Himself, a problem is presented to Him by the fact of His own indestructibility; 'To act or not to act.

[page 9]

[46] This fact is of such tremendous importance that we cannot do ourselves any disservice by repeating it over and over again until we have fully incarnated its significance in our own substance. Let us put it down again in as simple a form as possible. What the great religions have called God, in whatever language, is the indestructible infinite sentient power which is the creator, sustainer and destroyer of all forms whatsoever, in all worlds and times. This indestructible infinite sentient power, this God, because He cannot cease to be, is presented with the problem, 'To act or not to act', 'To do or not to do'.

[47] Let us try to conceive what this means to God. We will put it in the form of an imaginary conversation which God holds with Himself.

[48] 'I', says God, 'am infinite sentient power. I am not made of parts. I am a continuum, partless, seamless and eternal. I am, therefore, indestructible. I cannot get rid of myself, cannot annihilate myself. Whether I act or do not act, I remain my-self, infinite sentient power.'

[49] 'Because I am infinite, I cannot get away from myself, for, as the Infinite, there is nowhere where I am not. There is for me therefore no escape from myself.'

[50] 'As I am sentient I feel myself. If I act, I feel my action, its quality, its pattern, its intensity. If I do not act, I feel my non-action, its qualitylessness, its patternless formlessness.'

[page 10]

[51] 'As I am power, I can activate myself, formulate an infinity of forms, create endlessly worlds upon worlds upon worlds, universes upon universes. But as power I can also inhibit my creativity, oppose one action with another, neutralise my own formative energies, and hold myself in perpetual self-contradicting voidity.'

[52] 'If I, from my infinite power, act and create, I, from my infinite sentience, feel my own action and creation. If I act harmoniously, I feel harmonious. If I act discordantly, I feel the discordance in my-self. If I create beings which function efficiently, I feel their efficient functioning. Their successes are my successes. If I create beings which function inefficiently, I feel their inefficiency as my own. Their failures are my failures, their malfunctions mine. If I create beings which act mechanically, I feel their mechanicality as my mechanicality. If I create free beings, beings of free initiative, I feel their freedom as my own.'

[53] 'For each of my actions there is a corresponding feeling. For my inaction there is the feeling of nullity.'

[54] 'Some of my possible actions have feelings of pleasure, of happiness, of joy. Some have feelings of displeasure, of unhappiness, of misery.'

[page 11]

[55] 'If, therefore, I act, I have to face the problem of what kind of action I shall perform, for I shall feel its effects in myself. I shall be "mine own executioner".'

[56] 'If I refuse to act, I have no problem whatever, for a problem is an actual formal situation. But I have instead the feeling of non-action, the feeling of infinite power doing nothing, when it might do everything.'

[57] 'I have various possibilities of action and inaction. I may act simultaneously in a uniform manner throughout my infinity, or serially propagate a finite uniform motion-pattern through my infinity, or confine it to a finite locality, and remain inactive elsewhere. Or I may act simultaneously in various manners throughout my infinity, or serially

in various ways, formulating in some places, remaining formless in others. There are in my infinity an infinity of possible action patterns, or mixtures of action and inaction, propagated to infinity or finitely located. But whatever is actualised or not actualised, it is I who actualise or do not, I who feel it, I who suffer the consequences of my own decision or lack of it.'

[58] Having listened in to this conversation, it might occur to us to ask ourselves, in view of its import, what we would do if we also were infinite sentient power. 'To act or not to act?'. That is the question. The answer is simple. We can choose either to act or not to act, throughout infinity, or finitely. But whatever we choose it is we who will have to suffer the immediate and consequential results of our own choice.

[page 12]

[59] Having thought this through, it is not improbable that we shall say of God, 'He has our sympathy'. Certainly we have His.

[page 13]

[End of Chapter 1]

Books by and about Eugene Halliday

Published by Melchisedec Press (with ISBN Numbers)

All these books can be bought online or through your local bookshop.

The Collected Works of Eugene Halliday:-

Defence of the Devil—978-1-872240-00-8

Reflexive Self-Consciousness

    Hardback 1989—978-1-872240-01-5

    Paperback 2018— 978-1-872240-39-8

    eBook— 978-1-872240-40-4

The Tacit Conspiracy—978-1-872240-02-2

Contributions from a Potential Corpse

    Book I—978-1-872240-03-9

    Book II—978-1-872240-04-6

    Book III—978-1-872240-06-0

    Book IV—978-1-872240-07-7

The Conquest of Anxiety—978-1-872240-09-1

Essays on God—978-1-872240-08-4

Through the Bible

    Book I—978-1-872240-10-7

    Book II—978-1-872240-13-8

    Book III—978-1-872240-14-5

    Book IV—978-1-872240-15-2

Christian Philosophy

    Book I—978-1-872240-16-9

    Book II—978-1-872240-17-6

Further works by Eugene Halliday

The Paradoxical Ego, by Eugene Halliday and Zhu Kabere

Hardback—978-1-872240-32-9

Paperback—978-1-872240-33-6

Ebook—978-1-872240-34-3

Who am I? How do I relate to my environment? The ego can offer a stable reference to support our development or it can become a barrier inhibiting it. Drawing on insights from medical practice, philosophy and science, this book considers the role of egoic dynamics in the ongoing evolution of consciousness. We hope that it will contribute to the quest for insight into these profound questions which have been with us throughout our history.

Die Eroberung der Angst (The Conquest of Anxiety) by Eugene Halliday, translated by Christian Handschug

Hardback—978-1-872240-35-0

Paperback—978-1-872240-36-7

Ebook—978-1-872240-38-1

Den meisten von uns sind die Empfindungen von Furcht und Angst in manchen Lebenssituationen, und deren hemmende Wirkung auf unsere Fähigkeit mit anderen Menschen umzugehen und unser Leben zu genießen, wohl bekannt. In diesem Buch bietet Eugene Halliday praktische Übungen an, mit deren Hilfe wir beginnen können, diesen schwierigen Gemütszustand zu überwinden und ein glücklicheres und erfüllteres Leben zu führen. Der Autor stellt dieses Problem in dem Kontext einer umfassend holistischen und spirituellen Lebensauffassung dar.

Jede Seite führt den Leser weiter auf dem Weg zu einem ausgeglichenen eisteszustand, um mentale, emotionale oder physische Konflikte zu lösen, wann immer dies nötig ist. Ich empfehle dieses Buch als perfekte Literatur, wenn Probleme zu lösen sind.

John Zaradin, Musiker/Autor.

You may also enjoy this music memoir by a friend of Eugene Halliday

Personal Journey: John Zaradin in Conversation

Hardback—978-1-872240-29-9

Paperback—978-1-872240-30-5

Ebook—978-1-872240-31-2

This book is for readers who would reflect on, understand and come to terms with the contents of their own minds. It is for those who choose to value internal personal freedom and live within it.

John Zaradin

This beautifully told unfolding of John's life—boy to man, intellectual to visceral seer—subtly, delicately reveals the genius of Eugene Halliday, a man for all men and women—literally, music for the senses!

Barbara Pidgeon, author of 'Shakti Manifest'

Listen to Eugene Halliday's Lectures:

    For the Institute for the Study of Hierological Values (Ishval)
    www.eugenehallidayarchive.info/audio_ish.htm

    For the International Hermeneutic Society (IHS)
    www.eugenehallidayarchive.info/audio_liv.htm

    Lecture Transcripts
    www.eugene-halliday.net

Further Information

    Melchisedec Press
    www.melchisedecpress.net

    Eugene Halliday Association (Ishval)
    www.ehassociation.org

    International Hermeneutic Society (IHS)
    www.hermeneutic.co.uk

    Eugene Halliday, Artist: the Man and his Work
    www.eugenehalliday.net

    A collection of Eugene Halliday's written works together with the books he co-authored with Fred Freeman. There is also the personal recollection of an individual who knew Eugene from the age of eleven to Eugene's death, including the powerful effect Eugene had on his life.
    www.eugehenalliday.com

In addition, you can explore the Links pages on these sites.

Index

A

ability, response-, 45
Absolute, 13, 14, 17, 21, 23, 29, 30, 33, 35, 39, 40, 41, 42, 44, 47
  (works) through the relative, 6
  infinite, eternal, sentient power, 6
  is infinite sentient motion, 14
  motion as produced by the, 6
  of the philosophers, 39
  Sentient Power, 6, 25
  two poles of the, 40
absolute motion, 30
  functions of, 21
absolute sentient power, 47
act, 60
  absolutely unconditioned, 25
  discordantly, 61
  free, 25
  initiated by pure consciousness, 25
  mechanically, 61
  of perception, 37
  of reflexive self-consciousness, 27
  of will, 37
  or do not act, 60
  reflexive, 34, 42
  refuse to, 61
  resec, 27, 37
  simultaneously, 61
  To act or not to act, 59, 62
  without being determined, 25
  without regard to the benefit, 25
action, 38, 44, 55, 60, 61
  desire-impelled, 41
  mechanical mode of, 33
  non-, 60, 61
  re-action, 42
  recurring patterns of, 43
actions
  conditioned, 23
  Inclination-determined, 24
  mechanical, 23

activate, 61
activity, creative, 34
acts, original, 25
actualise, 62
Adam, Fall of, 31
adequate response, 27
  powers of, 8
aidos kinesis, everlasting motion, 10
Almighty, 57
Alpha and Omega, 7
ambition, 22
analyst-patient relation, 23
Anaximander, 10, 12
ancient world, 56
ancients, 34
animal world, 41
animals, 23
apeiron, 12
  limitless or boundless, 10
appearances, world of, 55
Aristotelian logic, 56
art, surgeon's, 28
assimilation
  -capacity, 45
  stimulus-, 8
attention, directional flow of, 38
attitude, ego-centred, 38
avoidance, 28
awareness, 7, 32, 33, 38, 54, 55
  definition, 2, 3
  is immediate, 9
  No philosopher has yet succeeded in defining, 17
Awareness, 1

B

be, 'To be or not to be', 59
become
  freed from the tyranny of material reactivity, 47
  liberated, 47

reflexively self-conscious, 47
truly oneself, 47
behaviour, 38
  conditioned-reflex, 24
  patterns, 27
being, 29
  actual, 11
  enlightened, 39
  idea of, 11
  what it means to be a, 11
beings
  free, 61
  motion-modalities, 11
  motions of rotation, 12
  source of all, 59
Berkeley [Bishop], 10
Bhagavad Gita, 59
birth, 54, 55
Blake [William], 32
blockages, emotional, 47
bodies
  material, 11, 36
  reference points for consciousness, 40
Bodies, 19
body, 28, 31, 46, 54, 58
  as a function of the continuum, 36
  finite zone, 16
  limitations of the, 41
  material, 32, 34, 35
  motion-complex, 40
  non-identity (of self and body), 28
  observer's, 19
  over-stimulation of, 28
  vehicle of experience, 57
Body, 27
Boll Weevil [folk song], 20
bondage, 22, 42, 47
born, 54
bound man, 22
boundless, (*apeiron*), 10
brain, 4, 8, 28, 37
Buddha, 42, 54

C

catalytic
  creative-consciousness, 7
  creativity, 32
cause, 14
causes, of life and enjoyment, 56
centre
  of every enlightened being, 39
  reference, 32, 46
change, freeing, 32
chaos, 58
charge, emotional, 20, 22, 28, 37, 38
choose, 62
Christ
  Logos-God, 42
  seamless garment, 59
Chronos, Saturn-, 7
circle, 13
complexes, repressed, 47
concept, 37
conception, 55
  change the ... quality of, 39
conditioned
  -reflex behaviour, 24
  reflexes, 26, 47
consciousness, 4, 32, 33, 35, 36, 40, 42, 54, 55
  & materialists, 4
  and will, 29
  Assuming the form of a thing, 39
  back-flow of, 39
  catalytic creative-, 7
  content of, 39, 45, 59
  contents of, 5
  evolution of, 8
  field of, 17
  identification ... with a body, 19
  identified ... suffers, 20
  identified with itself, 32
  is a catalyst, 21
  is that in which objects may appear, 9
  itself, 38
  loss of, 28

man's, 8
modifications in, 10
naked, 31
No philosopher has yet succeeded in defining, 17
objective, 10
of consciousness, 9
reference centre for, 13
reference point, 16
reference points, 40
reflexive self-consciousness, 7
released from identification, 21
seeks to control its content, 41
-self, 39
slavery of, 19
sub-, 29
symbols of, 33
terms relating to, 1
turning back on itself ...epistrophe, 27
un-, 29
Consciousness, 21, 34
is not an object, 9
of itself free, binds itself, 41
precise meaning, 55
contemplation, 33
content, of consciousness, 39
contents, of consciousness, 5
continuum, 36
cannot disintegrate, 35
has no parts, 35
motions of the, 36
seamless indestructible whole, 59
sentient power is a, 59
Contributions From a Potential Corpse, 52
conversation, 62
cosmic illusion, Maya, 21
create, 61
Creation, 31
creation, Prior to, 40
creative
activity, 34
catalytic creative-consciousness, 7
initiative, 34
creativity, 23, 25

catalytic, 32
cycle
involution-evolution, 41
of experience, 48
cyclic
impulses, 12
process, 40

D

David Mahlowe, ii, 52
dead
in one's sins, 34
state of the object-identified, 42
death, 31, 35, 54, 55, 59
Death, 34
decision, consequences of, 62
define, to indicate limits, 17
definition, logical, 30
depression, 41, 57
desire, 18
deus ex machina, 25
de-value, remove [will] stress, 21
development pace, continuously accelerating, 8
die
to disintegrate, 59
to sleep, 59
to the material world, 59
died, 54
dignity, 26, 36
disequilibrated man, 22
disintegrate, 54
disintegration, 35, 59
disorders, mental, 34, 35
displeasure, 61
dissatisfaction, divine ... leads us to resec, 41
dogs, Pavlov's, 24, 26
dragon, 56
dream, 39
dreams, 59
dualism, avoid falling into, 14
dying, 54
Dying, 59

dynamic relations, 13

E

eagle, 33
Eden, 5
efficiency, 55
ego-centred attitude, 38
ego-sense, 27
emotion, 26, 38
    unpleasant, 46
emotional
    blockages, 47
    charge, 20, 22, 28, 37, 38
    content, 22
    identification, 22
    resultant of experience, 22
emotional states, 32
    of the psyche, 39
emotionally-charged experience-records, 25
emotions
    flux of the, 44
    unpleasant, 45
energy, 19
enjoyment, 56
enlightened being, 39
Epistrephein, 33
epistrophe, 27, 31
equilibration, 22, 47
equilibrium, disturbance of, 20
escape, urge to, 41
Eternal, 40
eternal form, 44
Eternal Recurrence, 33
eternity, 44
Eternity, 36
ethical considerations, 37
Eugene Halliday, 49, 52
Eve, 5
events, temporal, 44
everlasting motion, *aidos kinesis*, 10
evolution, 12
    human, 27
    involution-, 42

    involution and, 40
    involution-evolution cycle, 41
    protoplasmic, 24
evolutionary process, 41
executioner, mine own, 61
exist, what it means to, 11
existence
    beyond consciousness, 10
    threatens man's very, 8
experience, 38
    cycle of, 48
    differences of, 55
    of life, 54
    records, 26
    -records, 22, 23, 26
    -records, emotionally charged, 25, 34
    Verbalisation of, 30
eye, 8

F

failure to understand, 55
fairy stories, 56
falcon, 33
fall
    first, 41
    into object-identification, 41
Fall, of Adam, 31
falling, into identification, 18
Father, 25, 48
    source ... of all beings, 42
fear, 45, 46, 47, 55
feel, 61, 62
feeling, 1, 2, 38, 55
    knowing-, 54
    -orientation, 20
field, 35
    in electronic theory, 2
    infinite, 2, 3
    of sentience, 2, 3
Firth of Forth bridge, 20
five senses, 55
flux, 30
fool, 32

forces, 59
form, eternal, 44
forms, 55
   verbal, 30
formulation, 31
free, 42
   act, 25
   self-determination, key to, 9
   will, 24, 25
free will, 25
freedom, 25, 38, 39, 47
   and human dignity, 26
   attainment of, 27
   key to man's, 39
   original, 21, 33
   real, 42
   retention of, 34
freeing change, 32
fruit, 56, 58
fruits, 24
function, is interfunction, 53

G

garment, seamless ... of Christ, 59
genius, 24
German words, 58
god, 25
God, 36, 60
   cannot cease to be Himself, 60
   Christ ... the Logos-, 42
   conversation, 60
   principle of free consciousness, 28
   the Self of selves, 44
   Word of, 53
God of gods, is the Absolute Infinite
   Sentient Power, 25
God's will, theologian's concept of, 12
Godhead, of the theologians, 36, 39
Goethe, 58
Gospel, John's, 30
government, self-, 43
grace, 24, 25
greatness true, 43
Greeks, 27

Grenfell of Labrador's story, 28
growth processes, 41
guarantee, 36

H

Halliday, Eugene, ii, 49, 52
Hamlet, 58, 59
happiness, 61
hate, 55
hawk, 33
heart, 44
heaven, 25
   equilibration of power, 32
   real, 47
Heaven, 22, 45, 46
heavens, temporary, 47
hedonistic, view of the universe, 18
Hell, 34, 45, 46
hells, private, 47
Hermeneutic, International
   Hermeneutic Society (IHS), ii
Hermeneutics, 49
Hermetic doctrine, 45
Hierological Values, Institute for the
   Study of Hierological Values
   (Ishval), ii
Hierology, 49
Hindus, 39
hope, 55
human being, fully developed, 41
human dignity, 26
human evolution, 27
humanity, whole effort of, 27

I

I and my Father are one, 6
idea, 38
ideas, 10
   of the mind, 44
ideational processes, serial, 32
identification, 20, 28, 31, 32, 33, 34, 35,
   41, 42, 43, 45
   break, 23, 39

consciousness ... released from, 21
   fall into, 31, 37, 40
   free from, 31
   mechanical aspects, 18
   non-, 20
   pleasure-pain aspects, 18
   problem of, 13
   release ... from, 38
   rescue onself from, 39
   tendencies, 21
Identification, 26
   cause of ... suffering, 20
identified man, 32, 43
IHS, International Hermeneutic Society, ii
illumination, 31
   metaphysical, 24
illusion, 15, 42
   cosmic, 21
illusory processes, 42
image, material, 33
immortality, 35
impulses, cyclic, 12
inaction, 61
inclination, 25
   cause of, 22
   conquering, 26
Inclination-determined actions, 24
inefficiency, 55
inertia, 28
   mass-, 43
   to overcome, 38
infinite
   motion, 40
   power source, 11
   sentient field, 3
   sentient power, 14
Infinite, 40, 60
   Motion, 13
inhibit, 61
initiative, 36, 61
   creative, 34
insight, 56
   metaphysical, 24
instinct, 41
integration, 59

intellect, 44
involution, 12
   and evolution, 40
   -evolution cycle, 41
Ishval, Institute for the Study of Hierological Values, ii

J

Jesus, 42, 47
John's Gospel, 30
Johnson, Dr., 10
joy, 59, 61

K

knower, 31
knowing, 1
knowing-feeling, 54
knowingness, 55
knowledge, 55
   of oneself, 31

L

Lao Tse, 42
Latin, 54
law, 31, 32, 37, 39
   against self-slaughter, 57
   free from the, 42
   not under the, 31, 34
   of life, 57
   of mechanical action-reaction processes, 32
   of serial presentation, 44
   under the, 31, 34, 37, 41
Law of the persistence of error, 46
laws
   formal and logical, 32
   of his own consciousness, 5
   of motion, 5
leben, 58
legends, 56
leib, 58
lieben, 58

life, 39, 56
  experience of, 54
  force, 36
  is a function of love, 58
  ordinary everyday, 24
  -process, 55
  real purpose of, 58
  situation, increasingly complex, 8
  tree of, 56
Life, 58
  implies love, 58
  is Love embodied, 58
light, 36, 39
Light, 31
limitless *apeiron*, 10
line
  of infinite curvature, 13
  straight, 13
loben, 58
logic, 31, 44
  Aristotelian, 56
logical definition, 30
Logos, 30, 44
Logos-God, Christ ... the, 42
loss, sense of, 41
love, 53, 55
  Life implies, 58
  Life is a function of, 58
Love
  is ... the actualisation of potentials, 58
  is the working for the development of the potentialities of non-being into being, 58
  Life is Love embodied, 58
lust, 22

M

machina, deus ex, 25
machine, 24
  extricate ourselves from the, 25
macrocosmos, 32
Mahavira, 42
Mahlowe, David, ii, 52

man
  absolute, 5, 6
  bound, 22
  disequilibrated, 22
  fallen, 7
  generalising, 5
  greatest misleader of, 19
  identified, 32, 43
  object-identified, 24, 44, 46
  particularising, 5, 6
  pleasure-pain mechanism, 19
  reflexively self-conscious, 6
  resec, 31, 32, 34, 44, 47
  truly great, 43
  unfree, 23
  universal thinker, 5, 6
  who begins to generalise, 6
  who lost both legs and arms, 28
  wise, 32
  wise old, 55
Man, 24
man's nature, female side, 31
martyrs, behaviour of, at the stake, 28
mass-inertia, 43
material
  bodies, 11, 36
  body, 32, 34
  image, 33
  plane, 33
  reactivity, freed from, 47
material body, 35
materialists, [& consciousness], 4
materiality, 5
Maya, cosmic illusion, 21
mechanical
  aspects of identification, 18
  mode of action, 33
  reflex, 26
  response, 25
mechanism
  pleasure-pain, 19
Mechanistic thinkers, 28
meditation, 33
melancholy, 41
Melchisedec Press, founded, ii
mental disorders, 34, 35

mental process, 33
mental states, 10
messengers, 53
metaphysical illumination, 24
metaphysical insight, 24
mind
    ideas of, 39
    lower, 44
mineral world, 41
mirror, 8
misery, 57, 61
misleader, greatest, 19
modality, of ... infinite motion, 40
molecules, of water, 15
motion
    (property of the Absolute), 14
    absolute, 30
    absolute ... of ... philosophers, 12
    all things as produced by, 6
    concept of, 15
    eternal, 59
    eternal, of God's will, 12
    everlasting - *aidos kinesis*, 10
    infinite, 12, 40
    infinite eternal sentient, 30, 44
    modes, 40
    of translation, 12
    produced by the Absolute, 6
    rotating, 12
    rotatory, 16, 17
    self-actuating, 40
    translating, 16
    two kinds, 10
Motion, 19
    Infinite, 13
    Sentient, 40
motion-complex
    finite body is a, 40
    of a rotatory nature, 45
motion-complexes
    experience of pleasure ... Heaven, 45
    painful and unpleasant ... Hell, 45
motions
    cyclic and non-cyclic, 17
    inhibited, 45
    of rotation, 11
    of translation, 11
Motions, of translation, 36
motivational research, 19
Mythos, 44
myths, 31, 56

N

nature of reality, 56
negative phase, 41
nerve impulse, 33
    afferent, 23
    efferent, 23
nervous system, 28, 32
Nietzsche, 33, 52
Nirvana, misunderstood, 47
non-action, 61
non-identification, 20
non-identity, of the self and the body, 28

O

obedience, 37
object, 18, 42
    Consciousness of, 8
    enslaved by the, 40
    return from the, 40
object-identification, 26, 27
    release ... from, 34
    releasing ourselves from, 26
object-identified man, 24
observed, 17, 18
Observed, 9
observer, 17, 18, 26
Observer, 9, 10
OBSERVER
    THE OBSERVER IS NOT THE OBSERVED, 8
observing self, 8, 17
orientation, feeling-, 20
origin, 54
    of our being, 4

P

pain, 18, 19, 26, 28, 45, 46, 55, 59
parables, 44
Parabrahman, 39
particles, 4
particularising tendency
    of the lower mind, 5
pattern, 55
Paul [Saint], 31
Pavlov's dogs, 24, 26
percept, 37
perception
    act of, 37
    change ...quality of one's, 39
    objects of, 44
perfect, 25
phantasy, world of, 39
phase
    negative, 41
    positive, 41
phenomena, 33
phenomenal world, 36
philosophers, 18, 39
plane, material, 33
planets, 33
pleasure, 18, 19, 26, 45, 46, 55, 61
pleasure-pain, 26
    aspects of identification, 18
positive phase, 41
possibilities, relational, 14
potentialities, 58
potentiality, 40, 58
power, 47, 61
    abolute sentient, 47
    eternal indestructible sentient, 59
    eternal, infinite self-sentient, 59
    eternal, infinite sentient, 59
    incarnating, self-embodying, self-
        objectifying, 58
    infinite ocean of, 58
    infinite sentient, 14, 62
    original sentient, 42
    right hand of, 42, 48
    sense of loss of, 41

    sentient, 31, 34, 35, 36, 54, 58
    Sentient, 33
    ultimate field of, 54
    will to, 52
Power, 14
    Absolute Infinite Sentient, 25
    Sentient, 40
power source, infinite, 11
praise, 58
problem, 59, 61
procedures, Psycho-analytical, 23
process
    cyclic, 40
    evolutionary, 41
    mental, 33
processes
    assembling and dissembling, 54
    serial ideational, 32
prodigal son, 6, 48
prophets, 53
protoplasmic evolution, 24
psyche, 22, 37, 38
    emotional states of the, 39
psycho-analysis, 24
Psycho-analytical procedures, 23
psychological
    terms, 18
    theories, modern [of
        'consciousness], 29
psychology, modern, 30
purpose, of life, 58

Q

question, 62

R

rabbis, 24
rational thought, 41
react adequately, 44
re-action, 44
reaction, adequate powers of, 8
reactivity, freed from, 47
reality, 59

nature of, 56
substantial, 56
ultimate substance of, 58
records
   emotionally charged, 26
   experience-, 23, 34
Recurrence, Eternal, 33
reference centre, 32, 46
reflex
   mechanical, 26
   on oneself, 42
reflexes, conditioned, 26, 47
reflexion, 31
   a binding back, or return to Self, 33
reflexive
   act, 34, 42
   movement ... of consciousness, 27
reflexive self-consciousness, 7, 27, 32, 35, 38, 43
   how to ... gain and retain, 37
   key to man's freedom, 39
Reflexive self-consciousness, 8, 33, 35, 47
relation, analyst-patient, 23
relational possibilities, 14
relations, dynamic, 13
relative, the, 42
religions, great, 60
re-orientate, 24
repressed complexes, 47
rescue, oneself from identification, 39
research, motivational, 19
resec, 24, 27, 33, 41, 42, 43, 44, 47
   abbreviation for reflexive self-consciousness, 8
   act, 18, 37
   basic rule for the attainment of, 8
   divine dissatisfaction ... leads us to, 41
   exercise, 38
   key to, 9
   level, 21
   man, 31, 32, 34, 44
   state, 16, 28
   To gain, 38
   To practice, 39
   without, 39
Resec, 36
resec man, 31
resistance, to imposed forces, 41
response
   -ability, 45
   adequate, 27, 44
   mechanical, 25
   taxism-, 5
responses, mechanically determined, 26
return
   from the object, 40
   to oneself, 31
right hand of power, 42, 48
rotation of motion, Without, 12
rotatory motion, 17
rule, 43

S

sacrifice, 53
Samson, 43
Saturn-Chronos, 7
Saviour, of the world from the world, 39
science, Modern, 56
sea, 15
   motion of, 40
seamless garment of Christ, 59
self, 27, 28
   loss of, 35
   non-identity (of self and body), 28
   observing, 8, 17
Self, 31, 35, 38, 40, 42
   (real) is a free-will consciousness, 29
   free, 43
   is consciousness itself, awareness, sentience, 8
   levels of, 30
   of all selves, 39
   of man, 42
   of the Absolute, 42
   real, 29, 31
   return to the, 39

Supreme, 36, 42
true, 47
Self of all selves, 47
Self of selves, God, 44
self-activating, 59
self-actuating motion, 40
self-awareness
    no value ... without, 35
    Not losing, 27
    retain, 34
    transcendent, 8
self-destroyers, 57
self-determination, 31
    key to free, 9
self-government, 43
self-realisation, 7
self-reflexion, act of, 33
Self-rule, 43
self-slaughter, against, 57
sensation, 1
sense
    data, 5, 44
    organ, 37
    organ, conditions what we know, 9
    organs, 5
    'to feel', 2
senses, 44, 56
sentience, 1, 2, 7, 17, 29, 32, 33, 35, 36, 38, 40, 45, 54, 58
    definition, 2
    is infinite, 45
    No philosopher has yet succeeded in defining, 17
    of the Absolute, 14
Sentience, 40, 55
    is not a finite object, 17
sentiency, 14
sentient
    field, infinite, 3
    power, 31, 34, 36, 54, 58
    power, infinite, 14
Sentient
    ... Power, 40
    Motion, 40
    power, 33
sentient power, 35, 36

separativity
    and illusory processes, 42
    phantasy of, 31
serial ideational processes, 32
serpent, 11, 13, 31
Serpent, 5
Shakespeare, 8
sheep, 43
shepherd ourselves, 43
shepherds, good ... and bad, 43
Shiva, 21
sins, dead in one's, 34
slave, 23, 42
slavery, 22
    rescue onself ... from, 39
sleep, 59
Socrates, 42
soldier, identified with ... a concept, 37
Solomon, 44
Son, His, 53
son, prodigal, 48
source
    infinite power, 11
    of all beings, 59
    ultimate, 58
    ultimate source of all beings, 3
spirit, 40
states, emotional, 32
static, 12
stimuli
    deprived of, 10
    objective, 10
Stimuli, 19
stimulus-assimilation, 8
subconscious, 45
    not ... non-sentient, 30
sub-consciousness, 29
subject, 18, 42
    identifies with the, 40
suffer, 62
suffering, 59
Suicides, 57
sun, 33
Supreme Self, 36
surgeon's art, 28
sympathy, 62

synaptic resistances, 23
system, nervous, 32

T

Taoist, 32
temple, which symbolises the time-play, 43
temporal events, 44
terms
    psychological, 18
    theological, 18
theologian, 24
theologians, 36
    Godhead of the, 39
theological terms, 18
things
    finte, 44
    relational possibilities of, 14
    simplest and most valuable, 56
    ultimate root of, 56
thinkers, Mechanistic, 28
thought, 55
    rational, 41
Time, 36
    serial presentation, 44
time process, 43
time-play, 43
Time-process, 44
tree, 32
tree of life, 56
trees, 24
troubles of man's world, 55
Truth, 10
truth, orders of, 42
twentieth century, opening of, 8

U

ultimate
    reality, 59
    source, 58
    substance, 58
unconscious, not ... non-sentient, 30
un-consciousness, 29

Unconsciousness, ... objectless sentience, 10
understand, failure to, 55
understanding, 55
unhappiness, 61
Universal, works through the particular, 6
universe, 21
urge to escape, 41

V

value, 35, 55
    rests in will, 21
    to stress by will, 21
Value, 20
values, intrinsic ... extrinsic, 20
vegetable world, 41
verbalisation, 30
    adequate, 30
Verbalisation, of experience, 30
view of the universe, hedonistic, 18
voidity, 61
vortices, 40

W

Want, implies deprivation, 23
watcher, 17
water molecules, cyclic motion of, 15
water, behaviour of, 14
wave form, 11
wave-form, 15
waves, 40
will, 55
    act of, 37
    and consciousness, 29
    free, 5, 24, 25
    frustration of, 41
    -stresses, 20
    withdrawal of, 27
wise man, 32
Word
    of God, 53
    the, 30

world
    ancient, 56
    animal, 41
    mineral, 41
    of appearances, 55
    of partials, 42
    of phantasy, 39
    of things, 42
    phenomenal, 36
    Saviour of the world from the, 39
    un-whole, 42
    vegetable, 41
worship, 25

Y

Yggdrasil, 32
Yogis, 21
youth, ill-informed, 55

Z

Zarathustra, 42
zone, 18
    of rotating motion, 13